# Live

# critical ma

**edited by david tushingham**

**photographs by simon annand**

Methuen

First published in Great Britain in 1996
by Methuen Drama
an imprint of Reed International Books Ltd
81 Fulham Road, London SW3 6RB
and distributed in the United States of America
by Heinemann
a division of Reed Elsevier Inc.
361 Hanover Street, Portsmouth, New Hampshire NH 03801 3959

All material is copyright. Full details are supplied in the
Acknowledgments on page 205.
Selection and introduction copyright © 1996 by David Tushingham
Photographs copyright © 1996 by Simon Annand

The authors have asserted their moral rights

ISBN 0–413–69780–0

A CIP catalogue record for this book
is available at the British Library

Phototypeset by Deltatype Ltd, Ellesmere Port, Cheshire
Printed and bound in Great Britain
by Cox & Wyman Ltd, Reading, Berkshire

**Caution**

Any enquiries concerning performance rights should be made to the authors' respective agents:

For *Blasted*, *The Strip* and *The Neighbour*: Casarotto Ramsay Ltd, National House, 60–66 Wardour Street, London W1V 3HP.

For *The Lodger*, *Hurricane Roses* and *The Clearing*: The Agency (London) Ltd, 24 Pottery Lane, London W11 4LZ.

For *The Present*: Judy Daish Associates Ltd, 2 St Charles Place, London W10 6EG.

For *A Vision of Love Revealed in Sleep* (Part Three): Gloria, c/o Lyric Theatre, King Street, London W6 0QL.

For *Dealer's Choice*: International Creative Management Ltd, 76 Oxford Street, London W1N 0AX.

For *Some Voices*, *Somewhere* and *Beautiful Thing*: William Morris Agency, 31/32 Soho Square, London W1V 2DG.

For *Revolver*, *Cat and Mouse (Sheep)*, *Can't Stand Up For Falling Down*, *Neville Southall's Washbag*, *Fearquest*, *The Fastest Clock in the Universe* and *Indian Summer*: A.P. Watt Ltd, 20 John Street, London WC1N 2DR.

For *Happy Land West*: c/o Methuen Drama.

# contents

# editorial

Plays tend by their very nature to be discrete entities. Every play, large or small, has its own aura of completeness, its own distinctive world characterised by what it contains and what it chooses not to contain. The prospect of a book made up entirely of parts of plays, of fragments rather than wholes, may therefore seem slightly perverse. However, allowing these discrete worlds to collide within the covers of a single publication is the most effective way of presenting an idea of what is happening in playwriting in this country at the present time.

We are in the middle of a controlled and sustained explosion. Not only are an increasing number of talented writers choosing to work in this medium, they are taking the form in a multitude of different directions at once. Some of those featured in this volume would even dispute that what they write are 'plays' at all. Yet whether they call themselves 'writers', 'playwrights' or 'theatremakers', producing 'performance texts', 'plays' or 'theatre pieces', they are all part of a literary culture which continues to flourish in the British theatre. Despite the considerable and justified enthusiasm within these shores for physical and visual theatre, the rest of Europe still tends to think that writing is the area where the British have the most to offer. The number of original theatre texts of outstanding quality being written and produced in this country is exceptional by comparison with other countries in Europe.

It's an intriguing thought that more people in Paris have seen a play by Gregory Motton than a production by Stephen Daldry and more people in Berlin know Philip Ridley's work than Deborah Warner's – if only because the contrast is so marked with the situation in London, where younger playwrights rarely enjoy the media prominence of directors or designers. There are many reasons for this but one of the more interesting ones is that original productions of new plays are increasingly confined to smaller stages. In the seventies and early eighties a whole host of writers, both established and not-so-established, were commissioned to provide plays for those wide open spaces on the main stages of both national and regional theatres. This isn't happening now.

There is a tendency to conclude that plays just ain't as good as they used to be, but the situation is not as straightforward as that. The playwrights who have emerged in the nineties, some of whose work is presented here, have begun their careers in a world where, like it or not, new plays are a form of chamber theatre. By confronting the unequivocal nature of this position and adopting a more mature and experienced approach to work in smaller spaces, rather than simply regarding them as a stepping stone to somewhere bigger, they have been able to evolve a strong new aesthetic, which remains with them even when they do occasionally put work onto larger stages before bigger audiences.

Put most simply, it's a question of whether you allow the size of the stage to dictate to you what you put on that stage. A new kind of dramaturgy comes into operation when a scene is written to be performed in less space on stage than it might reasonably be expected to take up in life offstage. Traditionally the opposite has been true – Tosca usually stabs Scarpia in a room which could easily be converted into a two bedroom flat – and in order to sustain an illusion on this scale actions and gestures need to be both clarified and heightened. When actors have only a few square yards in which to play a vast outdoor scene and the audience is fifteen feet away rather than fifty, a normal, everyday action will appear larger than life. This inverted perspective gives the audience an increased sensitivity to the fragility of the illusion which is being created for them. If the performers then start to do things which are by no means everyday actions while maintaining that illusion, it gives the audience an experience which is more intense – and because of that intensity usually more complicated – than they bargained for.

The writers featured here have harnessed this intensity to make their theatre a thrilling place to be. Their plays may not show such broad worlds as the 'public' plays which were popular in the seventies and eighties but they show worlds whose size is best measured in other dimensions: those of detail and feeling. Rather than adopt the approach

'This play is of vital importance to the nation as a whole' they prefer something more along the lines of 'This is very important to me. I hope it might mean something to you too.' In doing so they've been able to exploit the ability of chamber theatres to tackle more subjective and ambiguous areas, situations pregnant with a variety of different possible meanings.

Here they are perfectly in tune with an age and a society which has learnt to distrust large and simple truths in favour of smaller and more difficult ones. There is a quality about their writing which is denser and more vivid than the world we can all see outside the theatre. It's the quality which Ezra Pound defined as poetry, *dichten = condensare*.

The poetic nature of their work is often misunderstood as an indication that today's playwrights lack the level of political consciousness of previous 'angry' generations. Anyone with more than a cursory knowledge of the writers in this volume and their work will know that they have more than their fair share of things to be angry about but they use their work to explore a much wider range of emotions. The ratio of plays being written to the opportunities for high quality productions is such that most writers have to pack each piece with as much meaning as possible. Their next chance may be a while in coming. The richness of thought and feeling which these plays demonstrate comes from being written out of an urgent personal need.

Writing plays is no way to get rich. Plays get written because their authors want or need to write a play. An indication of the level of this want or need is the violence with which the play as a form is reinventing itself. What I find very interesting is the number of playwrights, how different they are from each other, and how well they write. Contemporary British playwriting is frequently criticised for the lack of a magnum opus. But is such criticism missing the point? Shouldn't we be celebrating the virtues of a medium where writers seem untroubled by the anxiety of influence or the desire to prove that they alone are the one great playwright whose work makes all the others redundant? Isn't it rather refreshing that plays (except for *The Mousetrap* and anything connected with Andrew Lloyd Webber) don't last for ever: they open, you can see them for a while and then they're gone again, to be replaced by another one which is different? Isn't it better that the theatre's development is sustained by strong work from a wide range of individuals rather than a few stars bullishly comparing the size of their advances?

Theatres are among the few places where we can still experience being a community in a society which is becoming increasingly edgy, divisive and adversarial. The pleasure of theatregoing starts with that of becoming an audience, of turning up somewhere with a group of strangers and everyone being treated entirely equally, irrespective of where you've come from or where you're going to. This quality is worth remembering when reading the pieces in this book because that is the context for which they were created. However distinctive and individual they and the people who have written them might appear, however fierce the words or actions they may contain, each one is the offer of an event where you can share something with people you did not know before. Their greatest enemy is indifference.

David Tushingham

# emily woof
## from *Revolver*

Emily Woof is an actress and director. She has written and
performed a series of solo performance pieces including
*Sex II*, *Sex III* and *Revolver*, commissioned by the Royal Court
Theatre. She has also written *Piano Man* for BBC Radio and
devised/choreographed *Drive* with Toby Jones for Chisenhale
Dance Space and *Anna Susanna Part III* with Ellen van
Schuylenburch for Rhythm Method at the South Bank Centre.
Her acting includes *Middlemarch* (BBC TV) and Juliet in Neil
Bartlett's production of *Romeo and Juliet* for the Lyric Theatre,
Hammersmith and West Yorkshire Playhouse.

**A young woman walks to centre stage and sits on an office chair in a single pool of light. She is JANE FRASER, aged twenty-six, a TV researcher. She begins to confide in the audience.**

I used to have this friend who had this friend who was in the Salvation Army. She came to visit him. They hadn't seen each other for years though at one point they'd been very close and she was just about to go off to Sri Lanka on another long trip, and I'd been to Tamil Nadu on a year off which is just across the water from Sri Lanka and I thought, how interesting. So I came along to meet her in the pub where they were having lunch. I remember, I was feeling particularly happy that day and I was looking forward to meeting her. It was summer, she was wearing a nice frock and she had lovely eyes. We talked about this and that, then I asked her what her work was. I already knew that she was a missionary, but I still asked her what she did and she said that she was a missionary and I asked her what that meant and she said it meant she went to people and talked to them and taught them how to read the Gospel.

I said, oh so you teach people how to interpret things? She said, yes, and talked about how the Gospels teach through symbols about man's relationship to God. I said, so you teach people how to make sense of what they see . . . and I quizzed her quite light-heartedly, but how do you know that your interpretation is correct? She said that she just knew. I don't think she really replied to the question. She wanted to get on with her lunch, but she was exercising patience, so I practised a bit of symbolism.

I said, well suppose God is this crystal-cut ashtray and I am the cigarette. Does that mean that God is a dumping ground and I'm burning out until I stump out in the crystal lake of his loving kindness? Or my yellowing fingers are daffodils among the tables and each cut-glass tray is a deep lake, which without warning is emptied by the anonymous hands of bar-staff who move like angels in aprons from room to room? My fingers could be daffodils which fly off into the night, their heads whisked off by the wind at closing time. How can you be so sure of your interpretation? I mean how can you want to inhibit people like that? I mean, that is . . . that is fascist. (*She is beginning to get agitated.*) How can you sit there and say those things? You're not saying them now so much but you will and how can you? I'm upset and disgusted. I mean that's how people are killed! . . . How people are segregated! How people in freak shows end up there . . . as fucking freaks! I mean no one is a freak for God's . . . evil the way you go on and on . . . Don't patronise me – you fucking Christian with your staring . . . I know what I mean! Yeh, yeh, I asked her, WHERE DOES GOD LIVE THEN? . . . and she said she felt God everywhere and I screamed and hit her in the face with the full weight of my arm.

And my friend, a close friend let's say, said I was being violent and unreasonable. (*She is beginning to raise her voice considerably.*) Violent and unreasonable? I said. Look how violent and unreasonable she is! He said, you asked her what her work was . . . I said I couldn't believe he was taking sides. I said I'm angry and I have every right to express it. (*She is now shouting.*) Look at her! My God! Look at her eyes! I've never seen eyes so . . . placid. They're like fish eyes. She might as well be dead! She might as well . . . (*Shouting and stabbing her finger in the air.*) YOU ARE a reptile! Your voice is foul! Your face is like a fucking Sunday and your eyes are like fucking frogspawn laid in pools of piss . . . you cod-fucker, you're fucking crying . . . and she was . . . crying.

**Pause.**

Anyway I used to get angry like that, and now I don't have to any more.

# sarah kane

## from *Blasted*

Sarah Kane was born in 1971. Her monologues *Comic Monologue*, *Starved* and *What She Said* have been performed by fringe companies throughout Britain. *Blasted*, her first full length play, was premièred at the Royal Court Theatre Upstairs in 1995.

**A very expensive hotel room in Leeds – the kind that is so expensive it could be anywhere in the world.**
**There is a large double bed.**
**A mini-bar and champagne on ice.**
**A telephone.**
**A large bouquet of flowers.**
**Two doors – one is the entrance from the corridor, the other leads off to the bathroom.**
**Two people enter – IAN and CATE.**
**IAN is 45, Welsh born but lived in Leeds much of his life and picked up the accent.**
**CATE is 21, a lower middle class Southerner with a South London accent and a stutter when under stress.**
**CATE stops at the door amazed at the classiness of the room.**
**IAN comes in, throws a small pile of newspapers on the bed, goes straight to the mini-bar and pours himself a large gin.**
**He looks briefly out of the window at the street, then turns back to the room.**

IAN: I've shat in better places than this.

**He gulps down the gin.**

IAN: I stink.
    You want a bath?
CATE: (*Shakes her head.*)

**IAN goes into the bathroom and we hear him run the water. He comes back in with only a towel around his waist and a revolver in his hand. He checks it is loaded and puts it under his pillow.**

IAN: Tip that wog when he brings up the sandwiches.

**He leaves fifty pence and goes into the bathroom.**
**CATE comes into the room. She puts her bag down and bounces on the bed. She goes around the room, looking in every drawer, touching everything. She smells the flowers and smiles.**

CATE: Lovely.

**IAN comes back in, hair wet, towel around his waist, drying himself off. He stops and looks at CATE a moment, who is sucking her thumb.**

**He goes back in the bathroom where he dresses.**
**We hear him coughing terribly in the bathroom.**
**He spits in the sink and re-enters.**

CATE: You all right?
IAN: It's nothing.

**He pours himself another gin, this time with tonic, ice and lemon, and**
**sips it at a more normal pace.**
**He collects his gun and puts it in his under arm holster.**
**He smiles at CATE.**

IAN: I'm glad you've come. Didn't think you would.

**He offers her champagne.**

CATE (*shakes her head*): I was worried.
IAN: This? (*He indicates his chest.*) Don't matter.
CATE: I didn't mean that. You sounded unhappy.
IAN: (*Pops the champagne. He pours them both a glass.*)
CATE: What we celebrating?
IAN: (*Doesn't answer. He goes to the window and looks out.*)
       Hate this city. Stinks. Wogs and Pakis taking over.
CATE: You shouldn't call them that.
IAN: Why not?
CATE: It's not very nice.
IAN: You a nigger-lover?
CATE: Ian, don't.
IAN: You like our coloured brethren?
CATE: Don't mind them.
IAN: Grow up.
CATE: There's Indians at the day centre where my brother goes.
       They're really polite.
IAN: So they should be.
CATE: He's friends with some of them.
IAN: Retard, isn't he?
CATE: No, he's got learning difficulties.
IAN: Aye. Spaz.
CATE: No he's not.
IAN: Glad my son's not a Joey.

CATE:  Don't c-call him that.

IAN:  Your mother I feel sorry for. Two of you like it.

CATE:  Like wh-what?

**IAN looks at her, deciding whether or not to continue. He decides against it.**

IAN:  You know I love you.

CATE:  (*Smiles a big smile, friendly and non-sexual.*)

IAN:  Don't want you ever to leave.

CATE:  I'm here for the night.

**IAN drinks. She's made her point.**

IAN:  Sweating again. Stink.
    You ever thought of getting married?

CATE:  Who'd marry me?

IAN:  I would.

CATE:  I couldn't.

IAN:  You don't love me. I don't blame you, I wouldn't.

CATE:  I couldn't leave mum.

IAN:  Have to one day.

CATE:  Why?

IAN:  (*Opens his mouth to answer but can't think of one.*)

**There is a knock at the door.**
**IAN starts, and CATE goes to answer it.**

IAN:  Don't.

CATE:  Why not?

IAN:  I said.

**He takes his gun from the holster and goes to the door.**
**He listens.**
**Nothing.**

CATE:  (*Giggles.*)

IAN:  Shh.

**He listens.**
**Still nothing.**

IAN:  Probably the wog with the sarnies. Open it.

**CATE opens the door.**
**There's no one there, just a tray of sandwiches on the floor.**
**She brings them in and examines them.**

CATE: Ham. Don't believe it.

IAN (*takes a sandwich and eats it*): Champagne?

CATE: (*Shakes her head.*)

IAN: Got something against ham?

CATE: Dead meat. Blood. Can't eat an animal.

IAN: No one would know.

CATE: No, I can't, I actually can't, I'd puke all over the place.

IAN: It's only a pig.

CATE: I'm hungry.

IAN: Have one of these.

CATE: I CAN'T.

IAN: I'll take you out for an Indian.
    Jesus, what's this? Cheese.

**CATE beams.**
**She separates the cheese sandwiches from the ham ones, and eats.**
**IAN watches her.**

IAN: Don't like your clothes.

CATE: (*Looks down at her clothes.*)

IAN: You look like a lesbos.

CATE: What's that?

IAN: Don't look very sexy, that's all.

CATE: Oh. (*She continues to eat.*) Don't like your clothes either.

IAN: (*Looks down at his clothes. Then gets up, takes them all off, and stands in front of her, naked.*)
    Put your mouth on me.

CATE: (*Stares. Then bursts out laughing.*)

IAN: No? Fine.
    Because I stink?

CATE: (*Laughs even more.*)

**IAN attempts to dress, but fumbles with embarrassment. He gathers his clothes and goes into the bathroom where he dresses.**
**CATE eats, and giggles over the sandwiches.**
**IAN returns, fully dressed.**

**He picks up his gun, unloads and reloads it.**

IAN:  You got a job yet?

CATE:  No.

IAN:  Still screwing the taxpayer.

CATE:  Mum gives me money.

IAN:  When are you going to stand on your own feet?

CATE:  I've applied for a job at an advertising agency.

IAN (*laughs genuinely*):  No chance.

CATE:  Why not?

IAN:  (*Stops laughing and looks at her.*)
     Cate. You're stupid. You're never going to get a job.

CATE:  I am. I am not.

IAN:  See.

CATE:  St-stop it. You're doing it d-deliberately.

IAN:  Doing what?

CATE:  C-confusing me.

IAN:  No, I'm talking, you're just too thick to understand.

CATE:  I am not, I am not.

**CATE begins to tremble. IAN is laughing.**
**CATE faints.**
**IAN stops laughing and stares at her motionless body.**

IAN:  Cate?

**He turns her over and lifts up her eyelids.**
**He doesn't know what to do.**
**He gets a glass of gin and dabs some on her face.**
**CATE sits bolt upright, eyes open but still unconscious.**

IAN:  Fucking Jesus.

**CATE bursts out laughing, unnaturally, hysterically, uncontrollably.**

IAN:  Stop fucking about.

**CATE collapses again and lies still.**
**IAN stands by helplessly.**
**After a few moments, CATE comes round as if waking up in the morning.**

IAN:  What the Christ was that?

CATE: Have to tell her.

IAN: Cate?

CATE: She's in danger.

**She closes her eyes and slowly comes back to normal.
She looks at IAN and smiles.**

IAN: What now?

CATE: Did I faint?

IAN: That was real?

CATE: Happens all the time.

IAN: What, fits?

CATE: Since dad came back.

IAN: Does it hurt?

CATE: I'll grow out of it the doctor says.

IAN: How do you feel?

CATE: (*Smiles.*)

IAN: Thought you were dead.

CATE: Suppose that's what it's like.

IAN: Don't do it again, fucking scared me.

CATE: Don't know much about it, I just go. Can be away for minutes or
months sometimes, then I come back just where I was.

IAN: It's terrible.

CATE: I didn't go far.

IAN: What if you didn't come round?

CATE: Wouldn't know. I'd stay there.

IAN: Can't stand it.

CATE: What?

IAN: Death. Not being.

**He goes to the mini-bar and pours himself another large gin and lights a
cigarette.**

CATE: You fall asleep and then you wake up.

IAN: How do you know?

CATE: Why don't you give up smoking?

IAN: (*Laughs.*)

CATE: You should. They'll make you ill.

IAN: Too late for that.

CATE: Whenever I think of you it's with a cigarette and a gin.

IAN: Good.

CATE: They make your clothes smell.

IAN: Don't forget my breath.

CATE: Imagine what your lungs must look like.

IAN: Don't need to imagine. I've seen.

CATE: When?

IAN: Last year. When I came round, surgeon brought in this lump of rotting pork, stank. My lung.

CATE: He took it out?

IAN: Other one's the same now.

CATE: But you'll die.

IAN: Aye.

CATE: Please stop smoking.

IAN: Won't make any difference.

CATE: Can't they do something?

IAN: No. It's not like your brother, look after him and he'll be all right.

CATE: They die young.

IAN: I'm fucked.

CATE: Can't you get a transplant?

IAN: Don't be stupid. They give them to people with a life. Kids.

CATE: People die in accidents all the time. They must have some spare.

IAN: Why? What for? Keep me alive to die of cirrhosis in three months' time.

IAN: You're making it worse, speeding it up.

CATE: Enjoy myself while I'm here.

**He inhales deeply on his cigarette and swallows the last of the gin neat.**

IAN: [I'll] Call that coon, get some more sent up.

CATE: (*Shakes.*)

IAN: Wonder if the conker understands English.

**He notices CATE's distress and cuddles her. He kisses her.
She pulls away and wipes her mouth.**

CATE: Don't put your tongue in, I don't like it.

CATE: Sorry.

**The telephone rings loudly. IAN starts, then answers it.**

IAN: Hello?

CATE:  Who is it?

IAN (*covers the mouthpiece*):  Shh.

(*Into the mouthpiece.*) Got it here.

(*He takes a notebook from the pile of newspapers and reads down the phone.*)

A serial killer slaughtered British tourist Samantha Scrace in a sick murder ritual comma, police revealed yesterday point new par. The bubbly 19 year old from Leeds was among seven victims found buried in identical triangular tombs in an isolated New Zealand forest point new par. Each had been stabbed more than twenty times and placed face down comma, hands bound behind their backs point new par. Caps up, ashes at the site showed the maniac had stayed to cook a meal, caps down point new par. Samantha comma, a beautiful redhead with dreams of becoming a model comma, was on the trip of a lifetime after finishing her A levels last year point. Samantha's heartbroken mum said yesterday colon quoting, we pray the police will come up with something, dash, anything comma, soon point still quoting. The sooner this lunatic is brought to justice the better point end quote new par. The Foreign Office warned tourists down under to take extra care point. A spokesman said colon quoting, common sense is the best rule point end quote, copy ends.

(*He listens. Then he laughs.*)

Exactly.

(*He listens.*)

That one again, I went to see her. Some scouse tart, spread her legs. No. Forget it. Tears and lies not worth the space. No.

**He presses a button on the phone to connect him to room service.**

IAN:  Tosser.

CATE:  How do they know you're here?

IAN:  Told them.

CATE:  Why?

IAN:  In case they needed me.

CATE:  Silly. We came here to be away from them.

IAN:  Thought you'd like this. Nice hotel. (*Into the mouthpiece.*) Bring a bottle of gin up, son.

**He puts the phone down.**

CATE:  We always used to go to yours.

IAN:  That was years ago. You've grown up.

CATE: (*Smiles.*)

IAN: I'm not well any more.

CATE: (*Stops smiling.*)

**IAN kisses her.**
**She responds.**
**He puts his hand inside her shirt and moves it towards her breast.**
**With the other hand he undoes his trousers and starts masturbating.**
**He begins to undo her shirt.**
**She pushes him away.**

CATE: Ian, d-don't.

IAN: What?

CATE: I don't w-want to do this.

IAN: Yes you do.

CATE: I don't.

IAN: Why not? You're nervous, that's all.

**He starts to kiss her again**

CATE: I t-t-t-t-t-t-told you. I really like you but I c-c-c-c-can't do this.

IAN (*kissing her*): Shhh. (*He starts to undo her trousers.*)

**CATE panics.**
**She starts to tremble and make inarticulate crying sounds.**
**IAN stops, frightened of bringing another 'fit' on.**

IAN: All right, Cate, it's all right. We don't have to do anything.

**He strokes her face until she has calmed down.**
**She sucks her thumb. Then.**

IAN: That wasn't very fair.

CATE: What?

IAN: Letting me lie there like that, making a prick of myself.

CATE: I f-f-felt –

IAN: Don't pity me, Cate. You don't have to fuck me 'cause I'm dying, but don't push your cunt in my face then take it away 'cause I stick my tongue out.

CATE: I-I-Ian.

IAN: What's the m-m-matter?

CATE: I k-k-kissed you, that's all. I l-l-like you.

IAN: Don't give me a hard-on if you're not going to finish me off.
It hurts.

CATE: I'm sorry.

IAN: Can't switch it on and off like that. If I don't come my cock aches.

CATE: I didn't mean it.

IAN: Shit. (*He appears to be in considerable pain.*)

CATE: I'm sorry. I am. I won't do it again.

**IAN apparently still in pain, takes her hand and grasps it around his penis, keeping his own hand over the top.**
**Like this, he masturbates until he comes with some genuine pain.**
**He releases CATE's hand and she withdraws it.**

CATE: Is it better?

IAN: (*Nods.*)

CATE: I'm sorry.

IAN: Don't worry.
Can we make love tonight?

CATE: No.

IAN: Why not?

CATE: I'm not your girlfriend any more.

IAN: Will you be my girlfriend again?

CATE: I can't.

IAN: Why not?

CATE: I told Shaun I'd be his.

IAN: Have you slept with him?

CATE: No.

IAN: Slept with me before. You're more mine than his.

CATE: I'm not.

IAN: What was that about then, wanking me off?

CATE: I d-d-d-d-

IAN: Sorry. Pressure, pressure. I love you, that's all.

CATE: You were horrible to me.

IAN: I wasn't.

CATE: Stopped phoning me, never said why.

IAN: It was difficult, Cate.

CATE: Because I haven't got a job?

IAN: No, pet, not that.

CATE: Because of my brother?

IAN: No, no, Cate. Leave it now.

CATE: That's not fair.

IAN: I said leave it.

**He reaches for his gun.**
**There is a knock at the door.**
**IAN starts, then goes to answer it.**

IAN: I'm not going to hurt you, just leave it. And keep quiet. It'll only be Sooty after something.

CATE: Andrew.

IAN: What do you want to know a conker's name for?

CATE: I thought he was nice.

IAN: After a bit of black meat, eh? Won't do it with me but you'll go with a whodat.

CATE: You're horrible.

IAN: Cate, love. I'm trying to look after you. Stop you getting hurt.

CATE: You hurt me.

IAN: No, I love you.

CATE: Stopped loving me.

IAN: I've told you to leave that.
Now.

**He kisses her passionately, then goes to the door.**
**When his back is turned, CATE wipes her mouth.**

# gregory motton
## from *Cat and Mouse (Sheep)*

Gregory Motton's plays include *Chicken, Ambulance, Downfall, Looking At You (revived) Again, A Message for the Broken Hearted, The Life of St Fanny by Herself, The Terrible Voice of Satan* and *The Forest of Mirrors*. He has also translated Büchner's *Woyzeck* and several plays by Strindberg. *Cat and Mouse (Sheep)* was first performed at the Petit Odéon, Paris, in April 1995 and will receive its British première at the Gate Theatre, Notting Hill, in 1996.

UNCLE: Your majesty I have been watching the progress of the royal policy

GENGIS: Which one?

UNCLE: That of equity for all, fairness, lies, deceit, the abolition of words and a lot of money for your majesty

GENGIS: Yes

UNCLE: And I have observed its absolute success

GENGIS: Are my people happy?

UNCLE: There is a rosy glow about them to be sure (*Aside.*) on their little bottoms

GENGIS: Good. Then it is time for phase two

UNCLE: What is that?

GENGIS: A lock-out, a block-out, an eclipse of the sun and moon, drown their pets, bring me their women

UNCLE: Most prudent

GENGIS: Uncle

UNCLE: Yes Matty

GENGIS: Who are these people. . . My subjects

UNCLE: A most unworthy bunch. One of them is a dentist, several million do nothing at all. Another is a kind of . . . housing officer

GENGIS: . . . Hmm that last one, bring her to me

UNCLE: She cannot be moved. The whole economy would grind to a halt

GENGIS: Then we shall go to her. Where does she live?

UNCLE: In the house your majesty

GENGIS: THE house. Is there but one?

UNCLE: For the moment sire. Building is underway

GENGIS: But where do the rest of my people live?

UNCLE: In YOUR house gracious lord

GENGIS: What if I want to sell?

UNCLE: Eviction is a top priority. Eviction and cleanliness make a nation great

GENGIS: Let them all appear before me then

UNCLE: They are . . . a little shy

GENGIS: Surely in a group they feel confident

UNCLE: They are shy and . . . a little ill

GENGIS: How ill?

UNCLE: Some poor souls are limbless, some headless, some bodiless

GENGIS: What bold disease has wrecked my population?

UNCLE: The disease of being too cocky by half, AND not knowing the answer to a few simple questions

GENGIS: Is there no cure?

UNCLE: We sent a team of . . . doctors in

GENGIS: The result?

UNCLE: We're still counting

GENGIS: Well are there any hands or feet that you could bring me, I must remain on familiar terms with my people you know

UNCLE: I will have Aunty bring a bag at once

GENGIS: Good. This state business has given me an appetite – please fart into my mouth

UNCLE: (*Does so.*)

* * *

GENGIS: Steady me Aunty, the inspiration is upon me again; I shall grant freedoms never before dreamt of. I shall make everything illegal

AUNTY: The opposition your majesty . . .

GENGIS: Don't mention them. They have no poetry in their souls, no philosophy, their arguments are based on a dilated fundament, they sit down too long in the draught and now they blame me. Withdraw their prescriptions!

AUNTY: Quick your majesty, a decree!

GENGIS: Open the prisons!

AUNTY: Your majesty?

GENGIS: Close the prisons

AUNTY: ?

GENGIS: Open them. Close them. Open them. Close them. Who can tell which is which

UNCLE: That is a paradox young master

GENGIS: No, it's a dilemma, but not for me. My words come and go with the wind

AUNTY: What a genius. His words have no meaning whatsoever

GENGIS: Oppress the lowly! Liberate the unloved

AUNTY: Frightening scansion!

GENGIS: What's bad is good, what's good is merely useful, green belt is red tape, red tape is blue riband . . . Aunty you are distant today, perhaps it is time once more for the royal bath

**Sound of a bath being run.**

GENGIS: Come on muckers who will join me?

**They strip.**

GENGIS: Uncle what is that legal document in your trousers?

UNCLE: Oh it's nothing, merely wrapping for my member

GENGIS: Please let me see it, take it out

UNCLE: I couldn't

GENGIS: I can see the writing on it from here. Whose names are they? Not your conquests surely

UNCLE: O great king I can conceal it no longer. It is indeed a testimony of loves borne towards me, not conquests though but subjects

GENGIS: My subjects?

UNCLE: It is a petition

GENGIS: It has a formidable length

UNCLE: They say I should snatch the crown from your head, they say the abuses of your regime are . . . so many they have forgotten them

GENGIS: All of them? Ungrateful wretches! What must a king do?

UNCLE: . . . so I drew up a list of them myself

GENGIS: Ah?

UNCLE: They are as follows: you have usurped the role of tyrant which properly belongs to . . .

GENGIS: Who's he?

UNCLE: Nobody knows. You have spoken only the truth and forbidden fibbing in your cabinet

GENGIS: True

UNCLE: You have forbidden the use of paper. You have fed and clothed the hypocrite and abolished dishonesty

GENGIS: Thank you. I was wondering if anyone had noticed that

UNCLE: You have bragged of your weakness in a most ironical tone

GENGIS: They cheered me for it too God bless 'em

UNCLE: You have pissed on the beach

GENGIS: It pissed on me

UNCLE: Industry has suffered: 100 per cent employment, 1000 per cent productivity, sales nil

GENGIS: National pride if you'll pardon me Uncle. The workers love me for it and I love them

UNCLE: You have housed the homeless

GENGIS: What statesman could do less

UNCLE: In a giant slum

GENGIS: In my own favourite city, in my own arrondissement, in my own house

UNCLE: And charged them exorbitant rents

GENGIS: (*Smiles to himself.*)

UNCLE: And in a swingeing piece of legislative villainy that humiliated the rich and disenfranchised the poor –

GENGIS: Ah the double-edged sword!

UNCLE: – You taxed all mention of the underprivileged

GENGIS: What a great burden was thereby lifted from the national vocabulary. A most revealing piece of statecraft

UNCLE: So, with the opposition now withdrawn into self-imposed exile of silence in the capital's northern suburb of H . . . you empowered the bootless herd with the right of requisition creating unprecedented shifts of population and a reversal of political allegiances

AUNTY: He is an evil genius

UNCLE: You see sire, they have sinned, you have sinned, we have sinned, I, . . . well I have corrected sin from my blackened soul and am now pure

GENGIS: Forget that now, I have something important to say to my people. (*Goes to his balcony. Returns.*) I shall tell them: Lords, ladies and gentlemen, forgive yourselves, forgive your brothers and sisters, forgive me, try not . . . try . . . have faith. Don't you think that is rather moving?

UNCLE: Yes it is moving. But I would like to move them in some other way. (*He manipulates his rolled petition with barely controlled ferocity.*)

**Exits.**

GENGIS: Aunty, I am afraid. The Kingdom once renowned for its modest charms has become a bunker where people perform deeds of darkness upon one another

AUNTY: Oh it's only their way

GENGIS: Their way of what?

AUNTY: Their way of saying (*With great sentimentality.*) 'we are people too you know'

GENGIS: Oh I see, and the murdering and torturing that goes on in our parks and woodlands for entertainment?

AUNTY: Oh it's only their little way

GENGIS: Their little way of what?

AUNTY: Their little way of saying 'sometimes we're lonely, sometimes we're afraid, sometimes we don't really know what is wrong; so we take someone and we pull their teeth out with pliers, then set fire to them, a little group of chums together, girls and boys, supportive, caring, no nasty words

GENGIS: What does it all mean Aunty?

AUNTY (*ferocious*): It means the devil is amongst us, put the boot in hard while you've still got the chance. Put bars up at your window, don't talk to yourself after 8 p.m., don't give an inch or they'll take a mile, string 'em up, cut them down. You see?

GENGIS: Yes, I see

AUNTY: It's just their little way of saying (*Baby talk.*) 'we're lost and lost and lost and lost and we don't know our way home.' (*More so.*) 'We want some more money.'

GENGIS: But wait. I want some more money

AUNTY: Don't interrupt. It's their little way of saying, we want free this free that and free the other

GENGIS: Bastards! Wait till I catch them

AUNTY: They want you to be their scapegoat

GENGIS: Do they?

AUNTY: They want to blame you for the piss in their lifts

GENGIS: But I'm a socialist. I would never piss in a lift

AUNTY: Perhaps you haven't explained that well enough. You must communicate

GENGIS: I'll make a play a book a poem

AUNTY: That way they'll all understand. They love plays and books and poems

GENGIS: But how? They're all so thick

AUNTY: We'll put it on television and call it Bingo Wingo Zingo Zam Powee

GENGIS: What if they come round to watch it on my TV set? I'm not having any of them in here, they all stink of air freshener. Do they wear toilet cleaner as perfume?

AUNTY: Yes son they do

GENGIS: Maybe it's too late to help them

AUNTY: Aaah don't say that. Imagine their little faces looking up at you with their big eyes 'please help us don't to be such ignorant Tory goons'

GENGIS: The bigoted swines. The thought of them makes me want not just to piss in their lifts but to shit on their brains

AUNTY: It's been done. They have done it to themselves. Out of sheer bloody-mindedness of course

GENGIS: Ha! So British. So land of hope and glory. So UK

AUNTY: Doesn't it make you proud to be not British

GENGIS: Yes, urgh! I'm half Maltese

AUNTY: I'm half Madagascan

GENGIS: I'm half Chinese

AUNTY: I'm half Indonesian

GENGIS: I'm half Polynesian

AUNTY: I'm half Melanesian

GENGIS: I'm half MALVENIAN

AUNTY: I'm supporting the African teams in the World Cup

GENGIS: I'm supporting India in the alternative World Cup

AUNTY: I'm supporting rabbits in the animal World Cup

GENGIS: I'm supporting poor little pussies in the World Cup for animals with electrodes in their little brains

AUNTY: I'm supporting animals that aren't in any teams because they are too sick because they've been eaten by doggies in the garden

GENGIS: YOU HYPOCRITE!

AUNTY: ?

GENGIS: You train your dog to kill the very birds in the trees

AUNTY: Only Bedause he's hungwy . . .

GENGIS: Remind me, what is it just their little way of saying?

AUNTY: It's just their little way of saying that when the suffering is all too much it's time to stop for a few moments of reflection, a little sadness fills your heart, you can't go on, a tear comes to your eye, a sob mounts inside your head chest throat your eye, your vision blackens, a whisper from far away says 'someone, please if there is anyone, please forgive us'

GENGIS: But Aunty why don't we all love each other any more? Has it always been like this?

AUNTY: I hope you don't think I'm old enough to remember?

GENGIS: Sometimes I get so depressed Aunty

AUNTY: What you need is something to cheer you up

GENGIS:  I know! The assizes! Justice!
AUNTY:  That's right. It'll put the colour back in your cheeks
GENGIS:  Bring in the first accused

# neil bartlett

## from *A Vision of Love Revealed in Sleep*
## *(Part Three)*

Neil Bartlett is a performer, director, translator, writer and founder member of the company Gloria, with whom he has also created *Lady Audley's Secret* (1988), *Sarrasine* (1990), *A Judgement in Stone* (1992), *Night After Night* (1993) and *The Picture of Dorian Gray* (1994). He has translated Racine, Molière, Marivaux and Genet, written two books, *Who Was That Man?* and *Ready To Catch Him Should He Fall* and is Artistic Director of the Lyric Theatre, Hammersmith.

*A Vision of Love Revealed in Sleep (Part Three)* is scripted for the original performers: Neil Bartlett, Bette Bourne, Regina Fong and Ivan.

When the audience enters the theatre, the space is dimly lit; smoke fogs the air, and the stage is hidden behind a huge red velvet curtain. Somewhere, unseen, a grand piano is playing; phrases of haunting, melancholy music. The lights on the audience fade to black; the red curtain slowly opens, revealing a wall of black fabric. Onto this are projected a sequence of captions, white letters on a night sky:

VISION

VISION: SOMETHING WHICH IS APPARENTLY SEEN OTHERWISE THAN BY ORDINARY SIGHT: PRESENTED TO THE MIND IN SLEEP OR IN AN ABNORMAL STATE

VISION: A PERSON SEEN IN A DREAM OR TRANCE

VISION: A PERSON OF UNUSUAL BEAUTY

VISIONARY:    I)  ONE TO WHOM UNKNOWN THINGS ARE REVEALED

II)  ONE WHO INDULGES IN FANTASTIC IDEAS; AN
UNPRACTICAL ENTHUSIAST

A VISION OF LOVE REVEALED IN SLEEP

a spectacle dedicated to the memory of Mr S. Solomon

As soon as this last caption comes onto the black curtain, there is a sweeping, sudden phrase on the piano, to the sound of which the black curtain falls. The stage can only be very dimly seen. The back wall appears to be painted gold; rising to the centre of the wall is a golden staircase. In front of it there are four posing platforms, giving the effect of a grand artist's studio. Also on the stage is a grand piano. The pianist is dressed in black; as he finished the last phrase he lifted his hands as if to continue, but has held them in mid-air, suspended, frozen. Also in the room is a semi-naked man, posed like an artist's model, partially draped in a length of dull red silk. His right hand is clutched to his breast, holding something. Silence.

A single naked lightbulb snaps on. In the darkness, the effect is of a bright light turned on too suddenly in a bedroom. The audience can now see all of the shadowy, abandoned artist's studio.

The man has powdered white flesh and dull red hair; the naked bulb is burning very close to his face. He looks as if he has been woken in the middle of the night; he speaks in the broken, sleepy way you do speak when, for instance, woken by a phone call at half-past-two in the morning.

NEIL:  What time is it? Is it late?

*Upon the waning of the night, at that time when stars are pale, and when dreams wrap us about more closely . . .*
Are we alone?
I was sleeping. I was asleep, I must have been dreaming. I had this dream, and when I woke up I could remember three things, and the first thing was
*'I sleep, but my heart waketh';*
and the second thing was
*'Many waters cannot quench love';*
and the third thing . . . the third thing was
*'Until the day break, and the shadows flee away.'*
*And I fell to musing and pondering upon these things and then, behold, there came to me a vision, and I was walking in a strange land that I knew not, and it was filled with a light I had never seen before, and I was dressed as a traveller. And so I set forth, dazed, and wondering, with my eyes cast down upon the ground, and I felt just as one who sets forth on a journey but who knows not yet its goal;*
I didn't know where I was supposed to be going. And so . . .
*I called upon my spirit to make itself clearer to me, and to show me, as in a glass what it was I sought;* to show me what I was supposed to be looking for. *Then the silence of the night was broken, and for a short while I knew nothing . . .*
and then I looked up, and there was someone standing there. Standing right there beside me.

**NEIL unwraps what he is carrying in his arms and lets the red silk drape fall to the floor. This reveals that he is entirely naked, and that his whole body is shaved and powdered. He has been carrying a portrait; this he now shows to the audience.**

NEIL: This is a picture of Mr Simeon Solomon, born in London in 1840, in the nineteenth century. He died here, in London, in 1905, in the twentieth century, in our century. Mr Solomon was short, fat, thin-legged . . . ugly; everybody said so, ugly. Alcoholic. Redhaired. Bald. Criminal. Homosexual. Jewish – and this night is dedicated to him. Of all the lives I could cry for, tonight it is him I choose to mourn; and of all the men I could choose to follow; it is him I choose to follow tonight, on this night of all nights.

**NEIL's voice suddenly cuts from the elevated, gentle tone of the opening to a common, chatty, sexy conversation with the men in the audience.**

NEIL:  I don't know why I do it. It's just something I do. I follow strange
men sometimes. I see some man walking down the street, he gets on the
bus, I get on the bus too, it makes me late for work, it gets me into all
kinds of trouble, I don't know why I do it –
Mr Solomon earned his living as a painter and this –

**NEIL turns and indicates the gold wall at the back of the theatre. It can
now be dimly seen in the lights; it is in fact a giant decayed, unfinished
canvas, its golden surface covered in fragments of Solomon's paintings
and drawings, angels, robed figures and sleeping men. Across the
painting, spreading out onto the walls of the theatre in gold script, can be
seen the three quotations from *The Song of Solomon* which begin NEIL's
first text.**

NEIL:  – this is one of his paintings.

**NEIL walks to the painting, and hangs the portrait of Solomon on a nail
sticking out of its worn and paint-spattered surface. Quietly, he bends to
kiss the portrait on the lips, and murmurs something in its ear which the
audience cannot hear. He turns again to face them, walks forward and
picks up a small, old red-bound book that has been left lying on the studio
floor.**

NEIL:  And he also wrote a book.
And this, this is his book. He called it *A Vision of Love Revealed in Sleep*. And
everything I say tonight is true, and everything I say tonight is written
here, in this book, and this book was published in 1871.

**He begins to read from the book; the phrases of the text are continually
supported, punctuated and interrupted by the piano.**

NEIL:  *And I turned to the one who stood beside me in my dream, lifting up my
eyes, the eyes of one who has ever sought, but not found; and I gazed full upon him.
And he spake unto me and he said:*

**The piano stops; NEIL looks, but cannot see the person who he has been
addressing in his dream. To the audience:**

NEIL:  He couldn't be here tonight.
I invited everyone I knew, anyone who I thought might know him, just
hoping he'd come. I suppose I thought somebody might bring him with
them. I even invited people I didn't know, as one does. I went up to

complete strangers and said excuse me, yes you, I'm sorry, I don't know why I do this, I've been staring at you all evening, I've been looking at you ever since the houselights went down, would you like to spend the evening with me; would you like to spend this night, of all nights, with me – But he isn't here. I went to find his grave but they told me, I'm sorry, we've no idea. We don't even remember his name.

So I put the flowers down on a grave without a name, just hoping it might be his.

I put flowers on his grave but somebody must have stolen them, or cleared them away, I couldn't find them. I sat on his grave and talked to him out loud, there was no one there to hear me, there was no one there whose advice I could ask –

*And so I turned to the one who stood beside me in my dream and he looked full upon me, and he said; I know him whom thou seekest, him whom we go forth to find. He only appears to those who grope in the waking darkness of the world; in visions shall he be seen of thee many times before his full light is shed upon thee, and thy spirit shall be chastened and saddened by what it sees, but it shall not utterly faint. Look upon me, and I will support thee, and in thy hour of need, I will be the one to bear thee up. Come.*

*And he took hold of my hand, and he led me along the shore of a dim sea lying at ebb beneath a mysterious veil of twilight. I could see that his lips trembled with all the unuttered voices of the past; but he was not crying. He led me forth, and then he turned to me, he looked at me, and he said:*

Tell me all about him. What's he like. Go on, tell me about him. What was he wearing? What did he look like? What did he look like – describe his face to me. Tell me his address; did he live near here? You see I don't know. I don't know. I used to know. We all knew. Everyone I knew was quite sure, but now . . . I don't know. I can't be so sure any more . . . I see some man and I'm not sure if I've been to bed with him. I see some man in the street and I know I've been to bed with him, I follow him, but when I touch him on the shoulders, when he turns and says, 'Hello' – I can't remember. I can't remember his name. I can't remember his address. I can't remember anything at all of all the things we said to each other, in the dark. I get a letter and I see from the postmark it was sent two weeks ago and when I'm reading it I think; maybe he's dead now. I read a history book and I think maybe they're lying to me. How would I know?

How would I ever know if he was like me?

Or if, if we met, he'd like me?

What was he wearing?

*Tell me all about him.*

What should I say when I meet him; how should we talk to each other? I mean, how did men like us talk to each other in those days?

Ladies and Gentlemen, I wanted to ask your advice. What I wanted to ask you was: Is there anyone here who remembers the nineteenth century? No? Oh well never mind . . .

**NEIL improvises a brief talk with the audience, breaks the tension, welcomes any latecomers, has a drink and returns to reading from the book:**

NEIL: In 1869 Mr Simeon Solomon very helpfully wrote me his autobiography. It is thirteen lines long, and he entitled it

*'A History of Simeon Solomon From the Cradle to the Grave.'*

*He was pampered. He had a horrid temper; he grew fractious; the family was wealthy; . . .*

everything was going to be all right

EVERYTHING WAS GOING TO BE ALL RIGHT

EVERYTHING WAS GOING TO BE ALL RIGHT

Have you heard this story before?

*At the age of sixteen young Simeon had already illustrated the Bible.* His favourite book in the Bible was, of course, (keep up, keep up!) *The Song of Solomon.*

**NEIL's voice changes into that of a preacher.**

NEIL: 'The Song of Songs which is Solomon's, beginning at the third chapter and the first verse, which is "I sleep, but my heart waketh".'

**NEIL's voice drops into a hushed, sexual whisper; snatching up the red silk from the floor, he plays both Bridegroom and Bride, turning and posing from line to line, echoing Solomon's sequence of drawings to *The Song of Songs.***

NEIL: *I sleep, but my heart waketh. Listen; my beloved is knocking at the door, and he says, Open the door to me my sister, my dearest, my love, my dove, my undefiled one. My head is drenched with dew, my locks wet with the moisture of the night. And she says; I have stripped off my dress for the evening – do you want me to put it on again? I have washed my feet for the night – do you think I should get them dirty? And then he reaches out his hand – oh, when my Beloved slips his finger into the keyhole, my bowels stir within me. When I rose up and opened up to greet my beloved there was myrrh dripping off my fingers; the liquid ran down off my fingers all over the doorhandle. And I rose up, and I opened up to my beloved, but my beloved had turned away and gone by. I sought him, but I could not find him. I called to him, but he did not answer. Night after night I lay alone on my bed, seeking my true love.* I called him, but he must have been out. I wrote to him, but he didn't write back to me. *And so I said, I'll get up, and I'll go out, out through the city at night, through its streets and squares and I sought for him* on Old Street, and on Poland Street, but still I could not find him; I called for him in the Market, in the Vauxhall and even outside the Coleherne at eleven-thirty in the evening God help me, but still he would not answer me. *And the officers, going the rounds of the city walls, they met me, and they surrounded me, and they abused me, and they stripped me of my cloak and I said* Officer, have you seen my lover anywhere? And no sooner had they left me than I found my true love, and I seized him, and I would not let him go, and I took him home, to my mother's house, and I said Mother! Mother, here he is.

**NEIL holds up his finger as if it bore a ring.**

NEIL:
*Wear me like a seal upon your heart,*
*Like a ring upon your finger;*
*For Love is stronger than Death,*
*Passion more cruel than the Grave.*
*Love burns up fiercer than any flame;*
*many waters cannot quench love,*
*And no Flood can sweep it away.*
Everything is going to be all right
Everything is going to be all right
Everything's going to be all right darling you can trust me.
*At the age of eighteen he was hated by all of his family* – surely that can't be true; everybody's mother loves them . . . *At the age of eighteen he was hated by all of his family, and so they sent him away.* To France. Unfortunately history does not record exactly what Simeon spent his time doing on the continent; the pages of his sketch book for that year are quite blank, but we do know that he returned to London in Disgrace, which is always the

sign of a good holiday. And so they sent him away again, this time to Italy, to study Art —

**Using the silk again, NEIL strikes a grand art-historical pose: The Artist's Model. During this sequence he begins to play ventriloquist, the voice moving between his own and that of the nineteenth-century polite society he is conjuring. The effect is of a solitary figure in an empty studio, but a studio crowded with absent people from the past.**

NEIL: — and in Italy he had sex with . . . one, two, three, four, five, six, seven, eight, nine, ten, eleven, twelve, thirteen boys . . . well he was there for three months. One of the boys had a face he would never forget. Back in London, everybody was talking about young Mr Solomon and his paintings, they said, Oh! *Such a striking face, what's his name? Where on earth did you find him? Tell me all about him.* Some people even bought his pictures and hung them, I suppose in their living rooms. What Simeon liked to paint best was of course boys . . .

**NEIL climbs onto one of the posing blocks and runs through a series of poses echoing Solomon's paintings . . .**

Boys draped in silk. Boys dressed up as women. Boys praying to God. Boys with wings, *Tell me all about him. What's his name?* He knew everyone, anyone who was anyone; he knew De Morgan, Morris, Burges, Swinburne, Pater, Rossetti, Alfred Lord Tennyson. One night he made his entrance into a particularly aristocratic dinner party dressed only in the flowing robes of a Hebrew prophet, reciting a hymn in a language which no one else there could possibly understand. Another night he ran around a house in Chelsea, in Cheyne Walk no less, stark naked, and screaming like a cat. *Aren't you going to introduce me?* He knew everyone, anyone who was anyone, De Morgan, Morris — *Oh Simeon, I see you're not on your own again tonight. Aren't you going to introduce me? What's his name?* Simeon Solomon was very unattractive. Like me. Simeon Solomon had red hair. Just like I do. When he was a young man he shaved off his beard to make himself more attractive to boys, and that made him a very bad Jew, and when he was an old man no one recognised him any more they didn't even remember his name and he let his beard grow long and filthy and matted and stinking and in fact he looked just like some dirty, old, Jew . . . But he knew everyone, anyone who was anyone, he went to all the best parties, no doors were closed to him, he knew

everybody's name, and they said to him *O Simeon, and who are you with tonight? Aren't you going to introduce me?*
*Tell me all about him.*
They said to him, *O Simeon, what would you like to be when you grow up?*
and he said
Drinker, Failure,
Soldier, Sailor,
Old Man, Poor Man,
Beggarman, QUEEN.

**The music is now rising under NEIL's speech. He begins to introduce imaginary guests to the audience; by the end of this speech he has climbed onto one of the posing blocks; he is then caught in a gesture of entreaty, as if he was indeed an artist's model posing for an invisible artist.**

NEIL: He knew everyone, anyone who was anyone; the studio was full of people; every night he was surrounded. He knew De Morgan, Morris, Burges, Swinburne, Pater, Rossetti, Alfred Lord Tennyson; may I introduce Sir Frederick Leighton . . . Sir Edward Burne Jones . . . Lady Burne Jones . . . all the little Burne Jones's all of whom, all of whom are now dead! He knew so many people, he knew so many men, but history does not record their names, I know nothing about them not even their names, I only know the names of two of his lovers and for the rest I know nothing, nothing, I don't recognise their faces, I don't know their addresses, I wrote them a letter but they wouldn't write back to me, I called them on the phone but I couldn't get through, I said I have to talk to you, I want to ask your advice, I want to spend the night with *you and not with anybody else*, I hold out my hand and there's nothing there;
nothing –
nothing –
there's no one there.

**At the top of the staircase, in the middle of the picture, a double door slowly opens. We see IVAN, BETTE and REGINA, posed in a tableau based on Solomon's painting of the angel in the fiery furnace from the *Book of Daniel*. They too have red hair and are in red robes; but their hair is in the Pre-Raphaelite style of Jane Morris or Lizzie Siddal, and their robes are floor-length, and are of heavy scarlet velvet. They have gold shoes and**

**heavy make-up. Behind them is a scarlet and gold painted heaven of flames and angels. They begin to descend, with music. BETTE leads them, singing Cole Porter's 'In The Still of the Night'.**

BETTE:
*In the still of the night, as I gaze from my window,*
*At the moon in its flight, my thoughts all stray to you —*
*In the still of the night,*
*While the world is in slumber*
*Oh the times without number*
*Darling, when I say to you, —*
*Do you love me, as I love you?*
*Are you my life to be, my dream come true?*
*Or will this dream of mine fade out of sight,*
*Like the moon,*
*Growing dim, on the rim,*
*of the hill,*
*in the chill*
*still of the night.*

NEIL: Tell me all about him. Please tell me. What he was like?

REGINA: *She was wicked. She was not as other men are. She hath mingled with the ungodly.*

NEIL: Did you ever meet him?

IVAN: Well I just better had because he still owes me that hundred and fifty quid.

NEIL: Tell me, did you ever talk to him?

BETTE: It was six o'clock; it must have been getting dark, because the gas was coming on . . . I was walking along Fitzroy Street; he was living at number 12 then. The windows were dark and so I continued down the street.

IVAN: I walked down the street to number 46 —

REGINA: Number 46 Fitzroy Street WC1 where on the evening of August 20th, 1884, Mr Charles Mason was married before sixteen witnesses to his lover Mr Alfred Taylor —

REGINA: Alfred! I wore the black and gold lace, it was beaded to buggery, and then the police burst in and dragged me screaming to Bow Street —

BETTE: The curtains were drawn. I turned right and right again onto Cleveland Street —

IVAN: Number 19 Cleveland Street; loads of soldiers. Last night, I was with the Duke of —

REGINA: How much d'you get then?

BETTE: One guinea.

IVAN: and he said, 'Jack Saul, call me Duchess' I said, 'Excuse me! Am I going in the right direction?' He said —

REGINA: Wait a minute, Bette, was the name of that café we used to go to, just off Monmouth Street —

BETTE: The *As You Like It*.

BETTE:    ⎫
REGINA: ⎬  **Barry Stacey**!!
      ⎭

BETTE: My dears, sandwiches for ever.

REGINA: And Quentin Crisp. Eighty-years-old and still tinting! An inspiration to us all —

BETTE: You know I had lunch with him six weeks ago in New York. He was telling me about the time he came through customs and they said to him, 'Have you anything to declare?' and he said, 'Only my sin . . .' so I walked all the way down Charlotte Street and right onto Percy Street and then I paused and I looked up at the window of number 15 —

IVAN: Number 15, Top flat, where in the summer of 1928 Mr Charles Laughton was living with Ms Elsa Lanchester. The police were downstairs with some boy; it was the first time, but not the last time —

REGINA: Charles sat Elsa down on the sofa in the front room and he said 'Elsa —'

BETTE: 'Elsa, I have something to tell you . . . are you listening? I have something to tell you . . .'

IVAN: Are you listening? Anyway, I turned left and crossed the Tottenham Court Road (excuse me for being so specific, but I shouldn't want anyone to get lost) —

REGINA: My dear, it's enough to confuse anybody

IVAN: So I turned onto Gower Street and there he was. Sitting on the pavement; the most beautiful boy in London. I recognised him from the paintings; he was his favourite model; he said to me, 'Go down six doors and turn right onto Chenies Street;' —

BETTE:  I had to ask a policeman, he said to me, 'You must be for number 16,' I said, 'Officer, how can you tell?' –
REGINA:  He said, 'They're all in there –'
IVAN:  He said, 'You won't be on your own,' –
REGINA:  So what time does this thing start then?
BETTE:  Eight o'clock.
IVAN:  What time is it now? Are we late?
REGINA:  Eighty thirty-four.
BETTE:  Oh well here we are. Good evening. Evening Nicolas.

**They say hello to the audience.**

NEIL:  Tell me how old you are.
BETTE:  Next Question Please.
NEIL:  Tell me, what are your names?
BETTE:  Bette.
REGINA:  Regina.
IVAN:  Ivan.
NEIL:  No, tell me your real names, I want to know.
BETTE:  'Bette''s about as real as I get.

# simon burke

## from *The Lodger*

Simon Burke was born in Newcastle in 1961 and is best known as a writer for television, having created the series *Chancer*, *The Guilty* and *Faith*. *The Lodger*, which he describes as 'a protracted howl of rage in a loose elastic structure', was his first stage play and won first prize in the 1992 Mobil Playwriting Competition. It was subsequently produced by the Royal Exchange Theatre, Manchester and Hampstead Theatre.

**The door opens on a small-town suburban bedroom. A man enters: WISE is deep in his forties with a calm exterior – phlegmatic with a slow burn. He is still attractive, in a rugged and physical sort of way, but obviously has no interest in fashion. He is shy and ill at ease as he turns to hold the door open for a woman:**

**LOIS is lost somewhere in her thirties but perhaps looks older – a good-looking woman who has, perhaps, had more than her share of troubles. She is dressed smartly, but not fashionably, for business.**

WISE: This is the room. Obviously.

**His accent is Southern working-middle-class. LOIS looks round. It is a poor little room, unloved and unlit. The fixtures and fittings are as cheap as may be procured anywhere and there are as few of them as possible.**

LOIS: And thirty quid a week, yeah?
WISE: Er, yes. If er . . . if that's all right . . .

**She looks round the room and sighs.**

LOIS: Well, it seems a pretty shit deal for living here but, what the hell, I need the money.

**He stares at her blankly. She smiles, which softens her careworn features.**

LOIS: It was a joke.

**WISE nods seriously as she sits down on the bed, testing it for squeaks. Her soft Merseyside accent betrays both an education and years in the gutter.**

LOIS: Who else lives here then?
WISE: Just me at the moment. And whoever takes the room.
LOIS: Mm. (*Sweetly.*) So what's the story?
WISE: Sorry?
LOIS: Why are you renting it out?

**Despite her affable charm, WISE is a bit taken aback by the question. It has a purposeful air.**

WISE: Well, I need the money. Temporarily.
LOIS: You don't work then? As such.
WISE: Yes, no, I do, but the mortgage and everything . . .

**She stares at him with a hint of suspicion.**

WISE: Things have become a bit tight recently . . . you know . . .

**She nods sympathetically as he trails off. She sits on the bed, relaxed and self-possessed. She has a distinct but understated sexual allure. She is aware of her body and knows how to use it. She is not using it on him yet.**

LOIS: So, what do you do?
WISE (*beat*): Well, shift work. It varies. I work nights mostly. Evenings. At the moment . . .
LOIS: Yeah?
WISE: Yes . . . Security.

**She pulls at the counterpane.**

LOIS: I might need to leave quickly.
WISE: When?
LOIS: Anytime. I have to be – **flexible**.
WISE: Right . . . Are you . . . er . . . ?
LOIS: You married?
WISE (*uncomfortable*): Not any more, no.
LOIS: Divorced?

**WISE looks faintly hunted.**

WISE: She died.
LOIS (*whoops*): I'm sorry.
WISE: That's OK . . . You're not from round here then?
LOIS: No.
WISE: From London?
LOIS: Temporarily.
WISE: You working up here?
LOIS: Yeah.
WISE: So you wouldn't be here long?
LOIS: Hard to say. Does the thirty quid include the questions?

**He looks at her, thrown.**

WISE: Well, obviously, if you're going to be living here, I want to know a bit about you.

LOIS: I want a room, not a relationship.

WISE: It's not that –

LOIS: I like my privacy.

WISE: I haven't done this before.

LOIS: I have. It's easy: I give you the money. You give me the key.

WISE: Right. Yes.

**She stands up decisively to change the subject.**

LOIS: OK. I'll take it.

WISE: Oh. You like it then?

**She can hardly believe he's serious. No one could like anything about this room.**

LOIS: Oh yeah, it's everything I'd ever hoped for.

WISE (*beat*): Do I gather you **don't** like it?

LOIS: It's all I can afford. Right now.

WISE: You want the room?

LOIS: I **think** that's what I'm saying. Yes.

**WISE nods: OK, OK. He takes a deep breath.**

WISE: Well, I do have a few more questions, myself.

LOIS: Oh?

WISE: Well, just a couple . . . er, what do you do? For a living. For instance.

LOIS (*genuinely puzzled*): Why? What's it matter what I do? I want a room, not a job.

**She looks at him blankly, puzzled. He's flustered, on the back foot. She massages her temples, as if trying to get rid of a particularly bad headache.**

WISE: Well, I'm asking what you do, just, because, to be sure you can afford the rent. That's all . . .

LOIS: If I couldn't afford the rent, why would I come here? I mean, you'd ask me for the rent, and I wouldn't have it and you'd throw me out and I'd have nowhere to live. Why would I do that?

WISE: Well . . . Yes, I suppose.

LOIS: Are you saying, you don't want anything to do with people on the dole, is what you're hinting?

WISE: No, not really, I hadn't thought.

LOIS: I mean, if it's a question of the Inland Revenue, is what I mean . . .

WISE: No, no. There's nothing below board about this.

LOIS: You seem a bit nervous.

WISE: Do I? No I don't.

LOIS: So you'll be declaring the income?

WISE (*the slightest hesitation*): Yes, of course.

LOIS: But you'd prefer cash?

WISE: There's nothing below board about this.

**He's uncertain whether she's playing with him or not. She smiles.**

LOIS: Right. I'm a researcher. Market research.

WISE: Sounds interesting.

LOIS: It's a job. It's not **supposed** to be interesting. I work when I like, choose my own times. It's OK.

**He nods.**

WISE: Researching what?

LOIS: I'm not supposed to talk about it.

**A moment.**

LOIS: I mean, a lot of landlords don't want unemployed people. In case their rent payments go on record.

WISE: There's nothing below board about this.

LOIS: I just like to know who I'm dealing with, that's all, nothing personal – just business.

WISE: Obviously. Business.

LOIS: OK.

WISE: OK. Right. References . . .

LOIS: References?

WISE: Yes . . . Bank, or employer . . . References.

**She looks up at him, half amused, half irritated.**

LOIS: I'm sorry, I've forgotten your name –

WISE: Wise. Andrew Wise.

LOIS: OK Andrew, what about **your** references?

WISE: What?

LOIS: Are you going to give **me**, for example, letters from two people who've lived here?

WISE: What?

LOIS: I mean, if anyone needs references, it's me that needs references not you, especially as I'm a girl. I mean I don't know **anything** about you. I don't even know this is actually your house. Do I? You could be anyone.

WISE: This is silly.

LOIS: Is it? I suppose women don't get raped any more. What a **relief**.

WISE: Well, this is the first time I've actually let a room.

LOIS: That's OK, I suppose. I mean, that's not suspicious. In itself.

WISE: It's not suspicious at all.

LOIS: It's just a question of trust.

WISE: It's just that it's **normal**, you know, references. It's what tenants give landlords. Usually.

LOIS: Is it? (*Sweetly.*) I mean, with respect, how would **you** know?

WISE: Well –

LOIS: Yeah of course, what a disaster **I** could prove to be, I mean, tell me I'm curious, I am, I want to know, what could I do to you?

**She stands up, bubbling over with nervous energy.**

LOIS: I mean, am I likely to ruin your career? Drive your friends away? Destroy your life as you know it? (*She pulls some money out.*) Here.

WISE: It's not that.

LOIS: What isn't?

WISE: Well, there's someone else coming to look at the room.

LOIS: Is there? You just made that up, didn't you?

WISE (*flustered*): No, no . . . I didn't.

LOIS: OK, who's coming then?

**He hesitates. She suddenly looks exhausted.**

LOIS: It's **such** a bad lie. I've come a long way and I think I deserve a much better one.

WISE: Thanks for coming. I hope you find somewhere you like. Suitable.

**She realises he is serious and stares at him, stunned:**

LOIS: Excuse me, wait a minute, I can't believe my ears, are you saying, is someone actually saying, I'm not good enough to live here? **Here**?

What sort of person isn't good enough to live **here**? I mean, look at this place, look at it. Who're you expecting to rent **this**? You think maybe Japanese businessmen looking for a pied à terre maybe, or Fergie and her mates looking for a little hideaway I mean what sort of person you expect here? I mean, I have clothes. I **wash**. Which seems to me more than you can reasonably expect for this room, is what seems to me. I've never heard such a lot of bollocks about a thirty quid room before.

WISE: Please don't make a fuss. It's just business.

LOIS: Sure, OK . . . I'm sorry. Look, I'm tired and wet and bad-tempered and I've nowhere else to go and it's late and it's raining. This is OK and I want to stay. Here, take the money.

**She holds it towards him, but he doesn't take it.**

WISE: I'm sorry. I don't think this is going to work out.

LOIS: You're thinking, maybe you and me, we've maybe got off on the wrong foot, is what you're thinking yeah?

WISE (*incredulous*): Well, maybe.

LOIS: It's OK, I don't hold grudges. (*She smiles.*) And I won't need a deposit.

WISE: Look, Miss –

LOIS: Lois.

WISE: I'm sorry . . .

**Her face crumples and she starts to weep. He simply can't cope with this.**

LOIS: Where do you want me to go?

WISE: I don't know . . . Where did you come from? Look . . . please . . .

LOIS: You want me to go back where I came from?

WISE: No, no – look . . . it's just . . .

**He trails off miserably. She looks up at him hopefully with tearful, mascara-smudged eyes, and sniffs.**

LOIS: Or do you want me to go to the Inland Revenue?

WISE: What?

**She dries her eyes miserably. She smiles tearfully up at him. He can't believe his ears.**

WISE: I've got nothing to hide.

LOIS: No, of course. It's just a question of trust.

**She puts the money on a bedside table. He looks at it, then her. The moment hangs. Then the phone rings. As if in a dream, he goes to answer it.**

WISE: Hello . . . No, er . . . the room . . . yes . . .

**The moment hangs and grows with his physical discomfort.**

WISE: No . . . (*A last painful pause:*) I'm afraid it's just been taken . . . Thank you.

**He puts the phone down.**

# richard cameron
## from *Can't Stand Up For Falling Down*

Richard Cameron was born in Doncaster and spent several years teaching drama in schools before starting to write full-time. In 1990 *Can't Stand Up For Falling Down* won him an unprecedented third *Sunday Times* Playwriting Award. His other plays include *Strugglers, The Moon's the Madonna, Pond Life, Not Fade Away, The Mortal Ash, Almost Grown* and *Seven.* His television play *Stone, Paper, Scissors* won the 1995 Dennis Potter Award. He is currently Thames Television writer-in-residence at the West Yorkshire Playhouse.

**Then. Eight years ago. Summer. A river valley.**

LYNETTE: I dropped down in the grass. Heard it like an Indian, coming through the earth, high up over the other side, coming up the lane to the top on the other side then winding down through the trees to the river and our bridge. Ringing loud like it was right here and then soft like it had gone into a hole in the ground and out again, nearer, louder, going through tunnels in the trees. I don't want it to be for us. Don't make it for us.

I see my mother in my head, back at the cottage, counting the roses on the walls, the tassels on the lamp by her bed. Dad must have run up the hill to the village. And she, waiting, crying in pain again, thinking of me in the field, fourteen, racing up the track to swing the gate open for them, worried. But I didn't. I lay down hard so it wouldn't see me and wished it away and even when it didn't come over our bridge and I knew it wasn't coming over the bridge, I still thought it would. They've gone down the wrong track. They'll stop and come back. Trying to trick me. Make me feel happy that it's for somebody else so I won't feel so bad when it turns out to be for us.

But it didn't come back. It kept on going and away, along the far side of the river, and I counted the quarries till I couldn't hear it any more. And I thought if it's for us, guide them back, don't be so cruel if you know it's for us.

But they didn't come back. Even when I knew it wasn't hers, I thought it was, and wouldn't let myself smile or laugh yet, like I wanted to, knowing I knew it was for someone else. Soon as I REALLY knew, I knew I would be laughing. I wouldn't be able to stop myself from being happy that someone else was ill, and I knew God would punish me and think me bad but I didn't care. I would fall out of a tree and break my leg and it would kill me and God would say, 'Serves you right for laughing at someone else's ambulance'. But I didn't care.

And then they came back and YES it climbed the side of the hill away from the river, through the trees, tunnels of trees, ringing loud and soft and away from me, over the top of the valley, away from ME, up now, crying and laughing in the field, dancing because it was someone else's ambulance and not my mother's. And I'm picking flowers for her, and I can see her when I give them to her and she's trimming and filling the vase and singing softly to herself.

RUBY: I knew for sure the day before Al Janney died.

Aunt Madge said so. I wanted to ask her about it, but didn't. We sat in her little back room by the window, the table full of brasses that I dulled and she polished, and after a while of me thinking how I was going to tell her, she said,

'Does your mother know?'

and I said 'Does my mother know what?'

and she said 'Getting yourself pregnant'

and I said, 'Who says I am?'

and she said 'Aren't you?'

And I dulled a little brass ship and said 'Don't tell' and she said 'I won't if you don't want me to.'

I told her what I could and my fear went away and came on again in waves, but mostly I thanked God to have someone to talk to and whilst we talked I dulled and she polished. She asked me who it was and I couldn't tell her. Not before I told him. Tomorrow I'd tell him.

It was the Saturday that Al died. The day I went to tell Royce, when I was eighteen and expecting his baby and I had to ask him what I should do and I walked to their shop and just before I got there, I turned off, back along Church Lane and round, and on our road again, and past our house and up to the shop and turned off the other way and Saturday morning I walked miles to get to their shop up the road and when I got there it was closed for dinner.

Al was looking in the window. He had a little girl with him. I went down the alley to the back of the shop, up the yard and I could hear the radio playing in the back room.

John Farrow, Kite and Royce were playing cards and drinking beer. He laid a card and looked at me and the look said enough to make me want to go, and it was his turn to lay again and I turned away and he said 'Come here' and I came to him and stood by his chair and his hand went between my knees and stroked the front of my leg where they all could see.

'Don't,' I said, and tried to pull away, but his hand held me fast and they smiled.

'Get us three pasties,' he said, and his hand that held me went into his back pocket and he put the money in my hand. I turned to go and he patted my behind.

I went to the butcher's and go them. Al and the little girl were still at Royce's shop front. He was flapping the letter box. I went up to tell him

to go but Royce opened the door and swore at him and pushed him away.
I gave Royce the bag and said 'See you tonight', and as he took the bag Al
dodged into the shop. Royce went in and tried to chase him out, cursing.
And I walked home.

JODIE: We never did more than hold hands, me and Al Janney. There
was only ever one kiss. I thought I was grown up. I was ten and he was a
lot older than me. I knew he was different. I knew he was still a boy in a
man's body.

I was in love with him. It was our secret. No one to know and tell me I
couldn't go around with a boy who was gone in the head, no one to tell
me it was wrong. But it wasn't wrong. We were happy. It went on
forever, like the river. Time was slow and easy and measured in laughing
and smiles and dandelion clocks and in Al Janney's eyes, and there was no
before or after in it to look back on and say 'we were happy then', it was
ALL now, and it was ALL happy.

We were married in May. I had the cotton and Al had all his pockets full
of all the sweet papers from all the streets in town, and down we went to
our hollow in the hill above the river and tied the sweet papers to the
branches of our secret tree, and so it became like sacred. And we laid
bluebells on our altar stone, under what we said was our stained-glass
windows that were dancing in the sunlight and I said I would love honour
and obey him as long as we both shall live amen and he said it to me and
we drank pretend wine from our silver-paper cups . . . and then he
kissed me.

RUBY: Sometimes it had felt good when Royce showed me off in front of
his friends. And their eyes when his hands were on me! And they would
laugh embarrassed and I was becoming a woman and we knew things
about love they didn't.

Walking home that Saturday afternoon I knew it wouldn't happen again
because NOW I was a woman and somehow my secret of what was inside
me wanted to make secret and private everything that was me and Royce,
and I was unhappy because I knew it wouldn't happen, and I knew it
couldn't be me and Royce and the baby, because there was my family and
his family and his life and his friends, and I cried because I had given him a
bag of pasties and a baby and he wasn't the kind of man to say 'thank you'
for either.

JODIE: That Saturday afternoon we went for a walk along the river bank.
We sat watching the barges. Three men came towards us. They had two

dogs. The dogs went down the bank for rats and slopped along the water's edge and came up again, dripping. Al saw who it was and said 'come on' to me and I looked and saw it was Royce Boland from the shop and two others. He had a big gun and I thought they must be after rats or rabbits. Al was up and walking off fast and said 'come on' to me again without looking back and I jumped up and caught him up and we walked fast and daren't turn round. Al must have thought they were after him, after they punched him in the shop and pushed and kicked him between them, and I nearly stumbled, we were almost breaking into a run, and Al said, 'It's them men'.

And now we were running and he held my hand to keep me with him and I looked back and they were running too and shouting and making the dogs bark and I felt some sick come up and sting my throat.

LYNETTE: I give her the flowers for still being here, and go out to Dad who's working the lock gates for a barge coming down. I'm happy because the bell wasn't ringing for her and she liked the flowers, but Dad is not happy and when I ask why, he doesn't say, so I don't know if it's Mother or me, or something else. And then he says 'youths messing about' and I understand, and think of the boy who they dared to walk across the weir for sixpence who slipped on the green slime in just an inch of summer water rolling over the weir top. Up went his legs and he crashed down hard and shot into the swirling suds and under, whirling in the strong currents, twisting and taking him away underneath while they waited by the weir for him to come up again and waited till they knew he wouldn't and ran the bank and the bridge and the other bank and both banks till they knew and went away and told the police who searched and searched and for seven days the town waited while men watched the river, but they missed him, and the next day his blue and bloated body popped up outside the power station, six miles downstream.

My father was one of the boys who dared him to cross the weir. So now he works the lock gates and respects the river and watches, and shouts at youths messing about who call him an old misery and laugh and swear at him from the far bank, but they don't know the dangers like him, and he gets sad sometimes, like now, because he was once upon a time a boy, and remembers how good it was, and how dangerous . . . and isn't now. And I think of the ambulance again, and look down at the water rushing from the chamber, look in my head for a drowned boy, stepped between a gun and a rat . . . and Dad has made me sad.

JODIE: Al could run like a rabbit but he had hold of me and I was only ten and I couldn't run any faster and holding his hand I was stumbling. Then a narrow bit of the path came up and we had to let go and I had to run behind him and he was getting further away from me. We were running up to the bridge and the road. I daren't look back. Al was at the fence by the bridge now and up, standing on the top, shouting. The dogs were nearly up to me. Then Al was down and up again with stones, throwing them at the dogs as I climbed the slope to the fence. And he was holding me as I jumped down into the road.

RUBY: I knew what I was. I didn't need anyone else to tell me. Speaks for itself, pregnant at eighteen. Walking round the streets and round again to get home that afternoon I tried real hard to feel as bad as I could, telling myself all the bad I had done, all the bad that was going to happen, thinking that if I brought it all into my head NOW and cried, and MADE myself bad, something . . . I don't know . . . something might be waiting at the other end with some goodness in it. Something to tell me everything was going to be all right in the end, even when it seemed everything was all wrong, something to show me it was worth going through all this, that everything was going to be all right.

JODIE: The black dog started to push through the fence. Al swung his boot to hit it in the side but it saw, and pulled back so he caught it hard on the cheekbone and it howled and went back to Royce who was shouting swearwords, running towards us with one of the other two. The third one wasn't there. He must have run up the hill to cut us off at the top.

RUBY: And suddenly Al came into my head, and how we used to make fun of him, taunt him, and him so daft and simple and laughing and desperate for someone to be his friend that he'd do anything for you. Like once Royce said they'd got him to lick up dog dirt before they'd let him play. I don't know if it's true – Royce has told me lots of stories – but we must have made his life a hell, and now I was thinking of him and thinking of what I'd done to him, and how I thought him a fool, and what laughs he'd given us.

JODIE: I'm running again. 'Wait. Wait for me Al!' He's a long way in front and leaving me. Royce and the other one are at the fence, and somewhere above us, cutting us off by the road that doubles back up the side of the hill, is the third one. Royce calls to him and his shout comes back through the trees and Al switches to the other side of the road and I see he's heading for the track that follows the river upstream, past the weir, to the quarries.

RUBY: And now, suddenly, in a rush, I loved him. A wave of his goodness and my cruelty washed over me, and thinking it all out was making me feel bad, like I wanted, and I kept it going and made myself remember . . . how I'd kissed him, how with Royce and the others we'd told him what to do with a girl and how I would show him and he came up to me and closed his eyes for ages and we fell about laughing and then I kissed him and Royce put Al's hands on me and I put my arms around him and pulled him to me and he must have been holding his breath because he pulled away gasping and red and we all laughed, but I knew I'd shown him something, felt his body shudder against mine, knew he was a child in a man's body.

And as I remembered, I thought how bad, how evil I was, and still am, and deserve it all, every bad thing coming. And then I knew that it was helping me, that I WOULD get to the other end, because I knew now that when I got home I was going to tell my mother about the baby. There would be hell in the house but it would be all right, because I deserved it. It would be all right . . . because I deserved it . . . because of Al Janney.

JODIE: Royce caught my hair and lifted me off my feet and then I was on the floor and thinking they were going to shoot me, head in the dust, my knees under me, begging them not to hurt me. And they pulled me up, made me stand up, and said, 'Make him come back. Scream. Go on', and so I screamed. 'Louder.' And I screamed louder and I could see Al a long way off so I screamed long and loud like they were killing me and I was crying and screaming and crying because Al was still running and they MIGHT have been killing me for all he knew.

RUBY: And when I got home I told my mother, because Al had made me, but it didn't happen like I wanted it to. She wasn't angry and screaming at me, 'You whore!' and packing my bags and Dad didn't get up and whack me. It was long, unbearable thinking silences that I didn't deserve when I wanted to be punished for what I was and what I'd done. She was wanting to help me and helping me made me feel worse and unworthy of her help. And yet . . . this feeling worse . . . as it was digging in to me, somehow it was scouring out all the dirt, and I DID know that everything could be all right even when it wasn't, and there was so much dirt in me, but she didn't mind, and I knew how much I loved her then, for the way she was cleaning me out, like the thousands of days of pots and pans, she kept on cleaning us out, making our hearts shine, knowing they'd only get used and bruised and black again, but she didn't mind.

I loved her, and Dad, and Al Janney, and Aunt Madge, who also spent her life shining brasses and hearts and in the middle of all my badness I knew there was something else, something good, because there were good people around me, and I wasn't alone, and my baby would be shown some love.

JODIE: I watched them go along the track and followed them. They went into the first quarry and sent the dogs to find him. Royce snapped the gun together, brought it to his shoulder and fired at the quarry face. The bang came back to me loud like thunder cracking and a swarm of jackdaws flew out and wheeled away over the top. Al wasn't there. The dogs knew.

LYNETTE: I waved the barge downstream, the dead boy and the ambulance still waiting in my head for me to turn round and look back at the lock and upstream to the weir and quarries. But I wouldn't.

JODIE: They went into the second quarry. Two shots went into the quarry face. Royce sat on a rock and smoked a cigarette whilst the other two clambered about with the dogs. Al wasn't here.

LYNETTE: I looked instead across the river, up the side of the valley to the clump of trees with the little hollow, where I found a tree that day with the sweet papers and the flat stone and knew it was a secret child's church that I had found, and left it untouched. I left it alone for the child to come back and play and pray.

JODIE: They went in to the last quarry, the biggest, canyon high, blasted rocks as big as houses against the cliff, higher than the sun. And the gun shots boomed into the cliff and boomed back, deafening, splitting and rolling in the air, as though a shower of rocks should fall with it, and the dogs hunted and the three men climbed and called and peered into caves between the fallen boulders, working their way around from one end of the quarry to the other, and I prayed that they wouldn't find him. Please God.

LYNETTE: And I wondered if she was there now, praying on the side of the hill, and would she mind if I, here, prayed with her for a while, to keep the good things in my life strong and clear, and the bad thoughts, the daydreams and nightmares waiting to throw a blanket over me and carry me away, dark inside and screaming – keep them down and locked away. Please God.

JODIE: Then I saw Al come out like a rabbit and make for the quarry face at the far end, and then they all saw him. The dogs barked and scrambled after him and the three men worked their way across the boulders towards him, calling, shouting, laughing, knowing he had nowhere to go. Then he started to climb, away from the dogs, fast at first, in a panic rush to get above them, then more slowly, stretching, moving into a steady climb, then more slowly still, as he went higher and higher, inching up and across, up and across, and they just stood and watched, and waited, and shouted, making him go on and higher in fear of them, a long time, until he was stopped and could go no further and just clung to the rock, high above them.

And I ran into the quarry and begged them to leave him. Please. He can't hang on any longer. He's stuck. Help him. And they laughed and waited and I kept saying please help him and then I think they got scared because he was stuck high up there and they didn't now what to do, so they pretended to be bored and went away with the dogs and left us.

RUBY: Tonight I am going to tell Royce about the baby, and I won't be scared of what he says.

JODIE: He was too frightened to move.

RUBY: I'm not scared. Al Janney has taught me not to be frightened.

JODIE: And then he fell.

RUBY: It CAN be all right, deep down, even when things are all wrong.

LYNETTE: Please God, I prayed, keep the good things coming. And it felt good that maybe a little girl was praying the same prayer as me across the river in her little secret church. And I was fourteen and needed a little secret church of my own, for there were things I still needed to know. Like would there always be joy and dread in my life? Will all my days have happiness and sadness together? Can there be one without the other? Can we know one without the other?

And the little girl, whoever she was, had made me happy again.

# kate dean
## from *Happy Land West*

Kate Dean's plays include *Down Red Lane* (Special Prize, Mobil Playwriting Competition, 1992), *England My Land* (South London Playwriting Competition Award, 1993), *Rough* (Birmingham Repertory Theatre, 1994), *The Stolen Child* (First Prize, Mobil Playwriting Competition, 1994) and *Happy Land West* (1995). She lives in Worcestershire.

**A crumbling stone barn. Centre a 1000 VF.**

HENNY **stalks out and is nearly ploughed over by** BOGGS **riding on** SCOTT**'s back. They career in with muddy hilarity.** BOGGS **is clutching four-packs in both hands. He's out of his face already.**

BOGGS: AMIGOS! AMIGOS!
SCOTT: Me back!
BOGGS: HENNY!
HENNY: Hey Boggsie 'ow yer doin'?

**She exits.**

SCOTT: I can' fockin' 'old 'im.
BOGGS: I'm back. Boggsie is back.
SCOTT: Get one o' them drums.

JESS **and** LENN **carry an oil drum over to** SCOTT.

BOGGS: Hey Shad my man. Whas wrong wi' Henn?
LENN: He owes 'er money.
BOGGS: So he owes me money. Careful!

**They hoist** BOGGS **onto the drum.** BOGGS **keeps his arm around** SCOTT**'s neck.**

BOGGS: He dropped me. Focker dropped me! (*Brings out cans from every part of his body.*) N' wot we got 'ere then eh? N' 'ere. N' 'ere. N' more. N' more.

BOGGS **screams in jubilation.** JESS **makes for a can.**

JESS: Alright!
BOGGS: You don' deserve nuthin. When did you las' visit?
JESS: The only way I go in there's on a stretcher.
BOGGS: Miserable bloody git. (*Gives one to* JESS. *Points at* LENN.) You!
LENN: Don' start on me man. I jus' got back.
BOGGS: Firs' stop big boy. (*Throws* LENN *a can.*)
LENN: Cheers.
BOGGS: N' my man. My fockin' man! (*Hands one to* SCOTT.)
SCOTT: Yer gotta be 'abstaineous' that nurse said.
BOGGS: Fockin' 'ate nurses. Are we ready Amigos?

LENN: Yeh!

ALL (*chant*): ONE AMIGO TWO AMIGO THREE AMIGO FOUR. FIVE AMIGO GET IT DOWN YER PUSSY BOY MORE!

**They crack open their cans simultaneously and neck them. BOGGS wins. He crushes his can and throws it at the barn wall. Opens another. Brings out a bottle of pills. Shakes the bottle. Swigs back a handful. Screams.**

BOGGS: Who wants some o' these? Get legless too eh?

**Through the blur BOGGS sees LENN and JESS staring at him. He looks down at his legs.**

BOGGS: Whas wrong wi' you? Hello. Hello. (*Laughs.*) Jus' fockin' look at em.

**JESS turns away and goes back to his bike.**

BOGGS: Eh big boy, I got some new wheels now. Faster than that crock o' shit.

JESS (*doesn't look around*): Yeh.

BOGGS: N' I gotta trick. Yer wanna see me trick Shads?

SCOTT: Wotta trick.

BOGGS: Yer gonna be jealous o' me. Ent they gonna be jealous?

**BOGGS brings out three coloured juggling balls and starts to juggle. He is fairly proficient despite his condition. SCOTT picks up the ones he drops. BOGGS sticks his tongue out with concentration.**

SCOTT: Are we impressed or wot? Beats macrami don' it.

**LENN and SCOTT watch hypnotised. JESS finally looks up but stays by the bike.**

BOGGS: Gi' it 'ere. I ent through me rep . . . repertoire. (*He changes to snatch juggling. His face breaks into a triumphant grin.*) I'm a star thas wot. I'm gonna sit up Edith Walk wi' the crusties n' make me fortune.

SCOTT: Me sister made em.

LENN: Wot's in em.

SCOTT: Pearl barley.

BOGGS: So's when yer starved yer gotta meal n' all.

LENN: Show us 'ow then.

BOGGS: Uhuh. Don' wan' you stealin' me livelihood.

**LENN studies BOGGS's technique closely. SCOTT goes over to JESS.**

SCOTT: 'Ow did that job go?
JESS: You was gonna gi' an 'and.
SCOTT: We can do it termorrow can' we. I'll come straight after milkin' if Rich lets us. That be okay?
JESS: 'Ave ter be won' it.

**SCOTT offers JESS a straight as a peace offering. JESS pulls a face at the packet. He puts them back in SCOTT's shirt pocket.**

JESS: Feelin' rich ent we?

**SCOTT lights JESS's fag.**

JESS: 'Ow is 'e?
SCOTT: He ent gonna walk again. Thas wot they said.
JESS: Wot do they know? They were gonna hack this off. Fockin' brain-dead bastards. They don' know . . .
SCOTT: Yeh . . .

**BOGGS takes a dive. SCOTT runs for him and hauls his ass back onto the drum.**

SCOTT: Whoa! yer alright?
BOGGS: YES! (*He cracks open another can.*)

**LENN takes over the balls and tries to juggle.**

BOGGS (*at* JESS): Hey Shads. Wot yer done this time?
JESS: Blew up mate.
BOGGS: Again? (*To* LENN.) Wot yer got now?
LENN: RX.
BOGGS: Very nice.
LENN: Very fast.
BOGGS: Best kip 'im off it. He ent good for bikes. (*He takes another mouthful of pills.*) I can' fockin' wait. I ent gonna walk so good but am I gonna ride.

**His mates watch him still and silent.**

BOGGS: All the bloke in the next bed could think o' was wot his girl was up to. Wot a thing ter worry 'bout. All I could think was gettin' out n' buyin' someat really big. I don't want no poxy RX if you've got one. Wot

I'm gonna screw out that fockin' Kev's gonna buy a Fireblade. Jus' like Johnie's eh? Ev'ry borin' fockin' second. Kip thinkin' Fireblade. CBR 900 R . . .

ALL: R R R . . . FIRE . . . BLADE . . .

BOGGS (*explosion of sound*): Gonna get me leg over that saddle. N' fock em all I'm gonna ride. I'm jus' gonna ride. There's me bubble see? Fireblade. Can yer see it? FIREBLADE! (*Dives.*)

SCOTT **rescues him.** BOGGS **wraps himself about** SCOTT.

BOGGS: Here's me legs! (*Throws the pill bottle at* JESS.) Go on big boy!

JESS (*reads label*): I'm immune mate.

BOGGS: Go on!

JESS **comes over and stuffs the bottle back into** BOGGS's **jacket.**

JESS: Yer 'ang onto them Boggsie.

BOGGS **gets** JESS **in a neck lock.**

BOGGS: Yer miserable bloody bastard!

BOGGS **ruffles** JESS's **hair.**

JESS/BOGGS: GET OUT OF IT!

BOGGS **lets him go and hands round the cans.**

LENN: Well 'ere we all are.

BOGGS: Less go. Less go.

LENN: We're back.

SCOTT: Yeh.

**Raise cans.**

BOGGS: We're back. We're back.

ALL: AMIGOS!

**They drink.**

# david farr
## from *Neville Southall's Washbag*

David Farr's production of *Slight Possession*, a devised piece
for his company Talking Tongues, won the *Guardian*
International Student Award and was seen at both the Royal
National Theatre and the Gate Theatre, Notting Hill.
Subsequent work as writer and director includes *The Detour*
(Gate Theatre), *Neville Southall's Washbag* (Finborough
Theatre), the devised show *Hove* (RNT Studio Springboards)
and *Les Grandes Horizontales* (RNT Studio), written with Rose
Garnett, in addition to productions of plays by Botho Strauss,
Strindberg and Gil Vicente for the Gate, where he was
appointed Artistic Director in 1995.

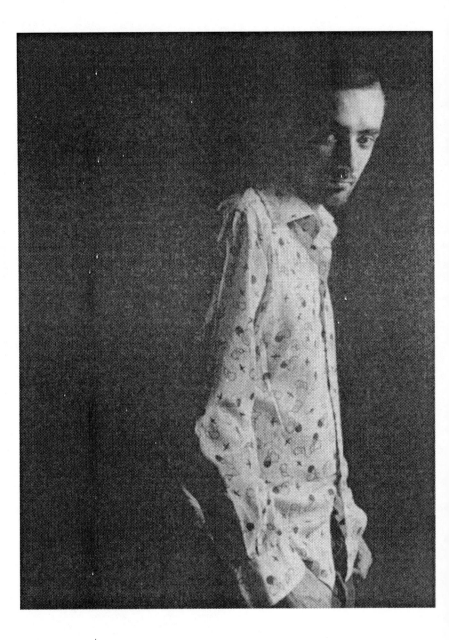

**BILL's room. An armchair. A television and VCR. Two doors. Boarded windows. BILL in armchair.**

**Night: BILL is avidly watching the television. Quite loud, we hear the commentary to the 1985 FA Cup Final's winning goal by Norman Whiteside. When the ball goes in, BILL suddenly rises up and gazes intently at the heavens. A roar from the crowd: 'United, United, United'. BILL stares ahead in triumph.**

**Then he sits, and the commentary is replayed in identical fashion. BILL's reaction is exactly the same. The procedure is repeated twice, but on the third replay, when the goal is scored the sound of the roar becomes deafening. A bright light. Then silence and . . . Black.**

**Lights up. Early evening. BILL talking to his television.**

BILL: He'll be here any minute. Look, it's just one night, he's my brother and I haven't seen him in a while, more than a while, he's my little brother and I like him, he used to sort me out, clear me up, so I owe him an ear and a bed. A bed for his band. They'll be gone in the morning. He's on his way somewhere and he'll be gone. That boy's going places. He's a natural at it, a real natural, a real quick learner, always was. He learnt the piano in a month. Eight grades in a month, all distinction. Seven years old. That's really good. His teacher was really impressed. Then he gave it up. Shame that, because piano's not just a matter of grades, but he never understood that. He always thought that once you'd done your eight grades that was it. You'd done it. But that's simply not the case. You see it's music. It's the swell of melody and rhythm. I used to say that to him, but he just looked at me all curious and asked were there any more grades. I think somewhere he lacked an understanding. He doesn't even play for the band. He's the manager, that's his thing now. Mind you, he always had a highly developed acumen. A tall man came round when my brother was four, looked at him, and said 'this boy has an acumen of startling potential'. Those were his very words. Can't remember what he said about me. But we got on, I remember that. I had quite a conversation on me for nine. But what he actually said . . . but we got on.

**A cuckoo.**

BILL: That'll be him. You just stay there all right. I'm going to the door now. You just stay there. The cuckoo door. I'm crossing my floor and heading for my doorknob. Now I'm here. I'm turning, I'm here . . .

**A cuckoo.**

BILL: I'm here I tell you.

**He opens.**

JIM: Bill.
BILL: Jim. You've come from home?
JIM: Leeds. Gig.
BILL: So you said. So you did. That's one journey. Miles of dark road.
JIM: Well not really, but the traffic was dreadful. You haven't been waiting. . . ?
BILL: Say I was. I wasn't but say I was. You're my little brother, little Jim, you've done more for me, you're worth every little second.
JIM: Yes.
BILL: You look good.
JIM: Yes.
BILL: You do.
JIM: I feel it.
BILL: You look it.
JIM: I feel good. Leeds was good.
BILL: Was it.
JIM: Leeds was the beginning.
BILL: I bet. But now you're down.
JIM: We're here.
BILL: I know that.
JIM: London.
BILL: She's a lady.
JIM: We're on our way.
BILL: You don't need to tell me that.
JIM: You'll like them Bill.
BILL: I'm sure I will Jim.
JIM: You'll grow to love them. They're not easy people. We're not easy. We're a band. It's not with a band to be easy. Yourself?
BILL: Change.
JIM: You?
BILL: Who else?

JIM: Stupid.

BILL: Real change. These few weeks I've been looking at some decisions, some stuff in my head. I've been clearing out.

JIM: That's good.

BILL: It is good. It's healthy. It feels it, you know.

JIM: Nice place. It's always been nice but this look . . .

BILL: Of course, this is new to you. I'm sorry Jim, I should have shown you round. I've become very reductive in my philosophy Jim. I think this room reflects that.

JIM: It does, yeah. So where did all the stuff go?

BILL: It just went out. What you see here is all I have. My two doors, my chair and my VCR. Having two doors just gives you that little variety. To know you can walk out on to two streets. Straight out through the front door. You see neither of them is a back door. Neither is a secondary door. That's important. They're both front doors.

JIM: How do you tell the difference then?

BILL: How do you mean?

JIM: Like when I rang, how did you know?

BILL: Cuckoo.

JIM: What?

BILL: You made a cuckoo noise. If you'd come in that front door, you'd have made a different noise. A warble. But you didn't. You chose the cuckoo. Where are the others?

JIM: They're buying stuff.

BILL: Band stuff.

JIM: Washing things.

BILL: Personal equipment, that's good. You sound organised.

JIM: You've got to be.

BILL: If you're going to be in a band.

JIM: You've just got to be.

BILL: You've got to be professional.

JIM: The days of the drugged-out hippy star are over.

BILL: Caput.

JIM: You've got to be on the ball these days. Or you'll miss it. There are people missing it every day. They don't even know it's gone.

BILL: That's what happened with this house.

JIM: Yeah?

BILL: Yeah, you know I began to not appreciate it any more. And one night it was gone. This woman came and took it all away. I came in and there she was tearing at the wallpaper with her nails. All methodical, like she was just getting on with her job. She wouldn't tell me who she was. Wouldn't even say how she got in.

JIM: Which door?

BILL: You understand.

JIM: I'm your brother.

BILL: She just kept ripping at the walls. The room was empty already.

JIM: In the truck.

BILL: Expect so. Funny girl. I kind of liked her in a way.

JIM: Body?

BILL: Shit no. She was a bit of a professional. She had these tremendously reliable fingers. I watched them for hours. Didn't miss an inch.

JIM: You still with that other woman?

BILL: Livinia.

JIM: Yes.

BILL: No.

JIM: I never met her. All the time you were together.

BILL: Nobody did.

JIM: But now it's over.

BILL: Yes.

JIM: That thing about her lips.

BILL: Dangerous. Like a bright light. You looked at them in the morning and they were with you all day. Burnt in your eyes.

JIM: So they've gone. She's gone. Change is good.

BILL: Still now. I still see them leaving. Livinia, did you walk backwards down the lane to hurt me?

JIM: Change can be rejuvenating.

BILL: Or to keep seeing me one more time? Did you still not want to go despite it all?

JIM: Where is she now?

BILL: I don't know. Changed her name to Libby. Disappeared.

JIM: And you're a new man.

BILL: Or an old one.

JIM: You're not old, Bill.

BILL: It's not the same any more, Jim. Being old doesn't mean the same thing. It doesn't take so long to get old any more. In the old days people used to die young, and that was sad in its way. But now everyone's dying old. This man I knew fell on a knife when he was twenty-four, but he wasn't young. He was really old. His skin was an old colour. These days you can get old in a couple of minutes.

JIM: It's where you are. London's old. But look at my skin.

BILL: No, but you're young. That's the thing, see. You're like that VCR. You're the latest thing, people are rushing out to snap you up and show you to their friends. But I'm like this chair here . . .

JIM: Scruffy.

BILL: . . . old. But however old this chair is, I still need it. I need it to watch the VCR. The VCR isn't the same without the chair. It's not as comfortable. And sitting in a chair all day with nothing to look at is uninteresting. Bare walls. So in this room I've managed a dependence. The old and the new are in harmony in this room. It took some honing, I had to get rid of a lot, but now I've found it, I'm not giving it up. A new feeling in an old chair, I'm at home.

JIM: Did you have to board the windows?

BILL: Yes, I had to, I absolutely and totally had to, all right? Christ, you wander down from some Northern ghetto, and in minutes you're getting at my home . . .

JIM: It's just a bit of light.

BILL: I've got a bulb haven't I? You having trouble finding your way around, groping are you in this murky twilight? Unboard the windows, that's really not going to interfere with my concentration, that's really not going to disturb my sleep, my time . . .

JIM: And what do you do with your time. . . ?

BILL: Take a wild guess.

JIM: We can find somewhere else. It's just one night. We're going places, we're not stopping for no moaning, wheezing . . .

BILL: Hold on, look at you, little Jimmy's lost his way, and he's all heated up. It's only a bit of fun, a bit of brotherly goings on, like, hold on, we'll get this right, this'll make you laugh . . .

BILL 'does the Harpo' on JIM. **This involves Harpo Marx's trick of feigning to shake hands and placing your acquaintance's hand under your thigh and smiling inanely.**

JIM: Oh God.

BILL: Ha ha ha, I love that, I haven't done that in years. I haven't seen those films in years. You remember, we used to watch *Duck Soup* all day, then go out and do it to everyone we met. To do the Harpo on someone, that's what it was called. We were irresistible. You remember that time you won that prize for being brilliant at something, this little woman who wrote poetry on mugs and socks came to present you with some award. And you did it to her. The Harpo. In front of the whole school. I still remember that. This little woman with a silver shield in one hand, and your thigh in the other.

JIM: They didn't give me the shield after that. I was denied my rightful prize. I wept. I swore I would never be denied again. I won't be.

BILL: Course you won't. It was only a shield. What does a shield do? Wastes shelf space. Stops doors. You weren't going to take it with you.

JIM: We're travelling light.

BILL: Good thing too. Instruments and wash stuff. That's all you need. You got instruments?

JIM: In the van.

BILL: You got a van?

JIM: Nice one. It's got facilities. Come and have a look.

BILL: No, I'm settled here now. Besides, I haven't shown you round.

JIM: Well, I think I get the picture.

BILL: No, hold on, you may think it's all pretty clear, but there's a history to this place. Each little turn, each mark tells a story. I'll take you on a tour.

JIM: No, it's . . .

BILL: Come on, don't disappoint me. This is an ancestral home. It's got tours. Right, this chair here you know about. I live here. I sleep, eat, watch the VCR here. This is where I start. I travel around the space, but this is my beginning and my end.

**Warble.**

BILL: Who's that?

JIM: **Warble.**

BILL: What?

JIM: That's the warble.

BILL: Yeah, but who's warbling? I wasn't planning visitors.

JIM: It's probably Tim and Shaun.

BILL: The band?

JIM: Yeah.

BILL: No, that wasn't a friendly warble. They're new, they'd announce themselves properly. No this is something else. This is an intruder. This person is already unwelcome.

**Warble.**

BILL: Pushy too. Well, we'll show him.
JIM: I'll get it.
BILL: No, let him wait. Let him suffer. I've had it with these people. It's time to make a stand.

**Cuckoo.**

BILL: What going on now?
JIM: That'll be them. I'll open it.
BILL: I'm under siege. I'm being attacked on all fronts.

**JIM opens cuckoo door. It is a WOMAN.**

WOMAN: Hello, I tried the other door but nobody answered.
BILL: Who is it?
JIM: I don't know.
WOMAN: So I went around the street corner to try this one. How amusing to live on the end of a street. Two doors. How entertaining.
JIM: Well, can I help you?
WOMAN: Yes, I'm collecting.
BILL: Who is it!?
JIM: She's collecting.
WOMAN: For the aged.
BILL: For who?
JIM: For the aged.
BILL: Tell her to get lost.
JIM: Get lost.
BILL: Tell her if she wants to help the aged, she can piss off. If she wants to help one aged person today, she can just get right out of his house. Tell her if she doesn't, then this particular geriatric is going to . . . O Jesus.
JIM: What?
WOMAN: Hello.
BILL: It's her.
JIM: Who?
BILL: The woman.
WOMAN: I'm collecting . . .

BILL: You took my house!

WOMAN: . . . for the aged. Could you supply a contribution?

JIM: What?

BILL: She took my house. You ripped off my wallpaper.

WOMAN: With my bare hands. Now, how about a contribution.

JIM: She did?

WOMAN: Just a pound.

BILL: And now she's back.

WOMAN: Fifty pence.

BILL: For more.

JIM: I thought you were glad.

BILL: I was, I was.

WOMAN: Everyone has given something. A small toy.

BILL: But now I'm raging.

WOMAN: A nominal donation.

JIM: You said it was all irrelevant.

BILL: It was. But look at her. She's enjoying herself.

WOMAN: Even small children can find something.

BILL: She's enjoying stripping me, hurting me.

WOMAN: Take this room.

BILL: You did!

WOMAN: This room must contain items not wholly essential to your welfare but which might save the life of someone less healthy and comfortable than yourself. This chair.

BILL: Get off it.

WOMAN: Whilst providing undoubted relief to your tired limbs . . .

BILL: Keep away from my chair!

WOMAN: . . . this chair would be a source of ecstatic satisfaction to an old man suffering from acute arthritis. Ask yourself do you need this chair? How often do you open that door? When did you last lean against that wall? How important is it to you?

BILL: Get her out.

JIM: How?

WOMAN: How important are all these things? Couldn't you live just as easily without them? And when you're old . . .

BILL: Just do it!

WOMAN: When you're not as fortunate as you are now, wouldn't you appreciate someone doing the same thing for you?

JIM: Look, here's a fiver all right.

WOMAN: Why separate that five-pound note from the other one you're keeping in your jacket pocket?

JIM: All right, have ten.

WOMAN: And why take them out of the jacket? What use is that jacket to you? Of course it's well designed, it's even rather stylish and à la mode but look into your heart and ask yourself, is it essential . . .

JIM: Yes it is.

BILL: This is my house.

WOMAN: . . . does my life depend on it?

JIM: Touch it and you die.

WOMAN: It might look unusual on a seventy-year-old woman, but isn't warmth more significant than appearance?

JIM: You keep back. If I lose this jacket, that's it. Over. Everything's just nothing. We'll never make it if I lose this jacket and if we don't do that, then we're nothing. We won't have made an achievement. I will do anything to prevent that from happening. I will take you and all the contributions you've collected and make a big fire. I will burn you to save this jacket. I will burn the aged to keep this jacket. And don't you dare tell me I've no sense of proportion.

WOMAN: Thank you for your donation of ten pounds.

BILL: She robbed my house. You're a burglar.

WOMAN: We'll call again soon.

BILL: Where's my stuff?

WOMAN: In the meantime, if you remember anything else you don't need, don't hesitate to call this number.

BILL: Don't let her go.

WOMAN: And you. I like you. Who are you?

JIM: His brother.

WOMAN: Call me, his brother. I've things to show you. Things of mine.

BILL: Tell her to bring back my stuff.

JIM: Bring back his stuff.

WOMAN: Now that was a contribution. A whole house. And he just watched me take it.

BILL: What's she saying?

JIM: She says you watched her take it.

BILL: I did not!

WOMAN: And he didn't say a word.

JIM:  And that you didn't say a word.

BILL:  Tell her she's a bitch liar.

WOMAN:  Not a whisper . . .

JIM:  You're a bitch liar.

WOMAN:  . . . passed his lips. His big, fat lips.

BILL:  What was that?

JIM:  She says you're gross.

WOMAN:  Not like yours. I like your lips. I like them particularly when you talk. Of achievement. They curl when you say it. They curl and turn. I want you when you say achievement.

JIM:  Are you coming on to me?

BILL:  What's she doing?

JIM:  She's coming on to me. Says she likes the way I say achievement.

WOMAN:  That was good. That time was really good.

BILL:  What is it with you and long words? Achievement, acumen . . .

JIM:  Look just leave all right. I can't . . . it's just the way my life is organised right now . . .

WOMAN:  Organised. That's really good.

BILL:  Do you find dictionaries attractive?

JIM:  Get off. I, I can't let you in, there's no room, it's a tight squeeze as it is, there's a tight squeeze in my life and I can't fit you in . . .

WOMAN:  I understand. I'll come another time. I'll appear when you least expect me. Meanwhile, thank you for your contribution. An aged person will bear a bright smile tonight; and that bright smile belongs to you.

**Exit WOMAN. Pause.**

BILL:  Has she gone?

JIM:  She's gone.

BILL:  Shame.

JIM:  Yeah. I liked her.

BILL:  What do you mean? You were all over the place. She had you all over. 'A tight squeeze in my life.' You were curtains. Ripped to shreds, you were, in front of your own eyes. I suddenly remembered how young you are. Hugging your desperate jacket. All of a sudden, you looked your age.

JIM:  Well, you really got through to her, didn't you, you really put her in her place. I bet right now she's rushing all over town to recover the stuff she extracted from your room . . .

BILL: Shut up.

JIM: She's probably in a real panic because of what you did to her, I mean you asserted yourself just then, and God you showed her a thing or two, she'll doubtless be screaming all over town . . .

BILL: Shut it Jim.

JIM: . . . just desperate to find every item and return it to its rightful owner because she knows if anything's missing you'll notice and you'll destroy her because you're so big and so wise and no one's going to cross big brother Bill, not when he's in that mood, and least of all a girl, I mean you could smell the sweat of woman, you could hear the whimpering. You could taste the fear . . .

**BILL overturns the chair and kicks and punches it.**

BILL: Shut up, shut the fuck up about the fucking fucker bitch! Look what you've done now you bitch, you've fucked the chair, you've fucked the fucking chair, how can I watch the television with no chair, the chair's upside down, my house is gone and my chair's the wrong way up, it's upside down!

JIM: So sit on it upside down.

BILL: What?

JIM: Sit on it. It'll make a change. It's only a chair.

**Pause.**

BILL: You're right. It's just a chair. It doesn't matter how I sit on it. I could sit on it like this.

JIM: Looks good.

BILL: Or this.

JIM: Great.

BILL: Feels great. You're right Jim. I'm too used to my routine. I'm too engraved. Like the television.

JIM: Same programmes.

BILL: Not even that. No, there's only one thing I watch any more. It's on my VCR. On that tape. That one there. That's what I watch. That's it.

JIM: What is it?

BILL: It's just this moment. FA Cup Final 1985. There's ten minutes to go, it's nil–nil, and United are down to ten men, Moran sent off, because the referee's fucked it up.

JIM: I think Shaun told me about that. He thought it was a pretty fair decision.

BILL: Well Shaun can fuck off, whoever Shaun is can go fuck himself, because the little, bald, crooked loser fucked it up. So, it's the seventy-eighth minute and Norman Whiteside's on a run for United. He's forty yards from goal, he's got the number ten on his back, Neville Southall is in the Everton goal – the finest keeper in the world. He hasn't put a foot wrong, it's not even a possibility. And propped up against the side netting is his washbag. Neville Southall's. It's got everything he needs.

JIM: What sort of stuff?

BILL: Everything. All those necessities. Neville's needs. So, Norman Whiteside's on the run, it's nil–nil, Southall's poised, the crowd's on the ball, the bag's propped up. There's nothing much on. He's got the number ten on his back and he's on his own. And Norman pauses, seventy-six thousand faces freeze, he looks up, and you can see, it's literally plain written across his face, he's going for that netting, he's going right for that washbag's zipper. He eyes it like an eagle, a hungry eagle. It's a left curler, he hits it perfect, Southall hurls himself, the finest keeper in the world, it's curling round, there's never any doubt, Southall's nowhere, there's no doubt, it's in, it's in the net, it's the cup for United, Norman turns, the crowd go wild, and the ball lands smack on Neville Southall's washbag. The ball is in. The cup is won. The washbag explodes. Neville Southall's necessities shoot into the Wembley air. His soap, shampoo and conditioner hurtle into the stands. His lens lotion, hair cream, his tubes of toothpaste, one fluoride, one Sensodyne, shoot out on to the pitch narrowly missing the celebrating players. Paul Bracewell, the battling Everton midfielder, leaps to avoid Neville's razor as it skims the Wembley turf. Everything else blows upwards – foot cream, boot polish, spare bootlaces, spare boots, canned heat, shaving cream, stick, foam, aftershave, roll-on, ointment, lozenges, sinus capsules, toothpicks, ear-plugs, cotton-buds, brush, comb, lipsalve, skin cream, moisturising lotion, sponge, flannel, towel, bathmat, gown, robe, dryer for his hair, powder for his nose, everything a man needs, a perfectly spherical pumice stone for his two verrucas. The Wembley sky is filled with the exploded contents of Neville Southall's washbag. Norman rejoices, Neville is inconsolable. It's the terrible miracle of football.

**Silence. Cuckoo.**

JIM: That'll be the band.

**Black.**

.

# phyllis nagy
## from *The Strip*

Phyllis Nagy was born in New York City and now lives in London. Her plays include *Weldon Rising* (Liverpool Playhouse/Royal Court Theatre Upstairs), *Entering Queens* (Gay Sweatshop), *Disappeared* (Leicester Haymarket/Midnight Theatre Company), *Trip's Cinch* (Actor's Theatre of Louisville) and *Butterfly Kiss* (Almeida Theatre). She was Arts Council playwright-in-residence at the Royal Court Theatre where *The Strip* was premièred in 1995.

**OTTO and KATE at KATE's office in Arlington, Virginia. KATE wears Walkman headphones. She carries a rather large purse.**

KATE: The leads you gave me don't check out.

OTTO: I felt certain they would.

KATE: Well they don't. What do you make of that?

OTTO: I haven't any notion. You are the reporter, Miss Buck. Report.

KATE: I wasn't an investigative reporter, Murphy. I was a columnist. There's a difference.

OTTO: Nonetheless. I hired you as a reporter.

KATE: I can't find Marquette. He's not in Roanoke. He's not anywhere in Virginia. Or in the Carolinas for that matter. Lynchburg cops got a positive ID on the prints found at the truck stop. And they are not Lester Marquette's prints.

OTTO: I believe they are.

KATE: I will not report false information. I have a duty to our readership.

OTTO: The *Arlington Pennysaver* is not the *New York Times*, Miss Buck.

KATE: It's still a newspaper. Even if it is a weekly. A free weekly. A free weekly shopper. Oh fuck. Why did I let you hire me?

OTTO: I seem to recall a rather nasty incident involving your ethics at the *Philadelphia Inquirer.*

KATE: I was duped.

OTTO: Pre-teen calculus genius with a crack habit plus disabled mum equals a prize-winning story. Heartrending. Metaphorical. And a fabrication.

KATE: I WAS DUPED.

**OTTO approaches KATE. He lifts up one of KATE's headphone speakers and leans in close to listen to what she's listening to. A beat, before he replaces the headphone in KATE's ear and steps back.**

OTTO: If the fingerprints aren't Lester Marquette's, then to whom do they belong? You said there was a positive identification.

KATE: That's right. It's positively not Lester Marquette.

OTTO: You favour sentimental popular music, Miss Buck.

KATE: I do not. I like . . . a little Motown, a little disco, this and that.

OTTO: The sentimental are always duped. In journalism as in life. I prefer jazz to pop. It resists false notions of a single shared experience and is therefore unsentimental. Your reportage has been flabby of late.

KATE: So I'm supposed to buy a Thelonius Monk tape and that'll fix it? I don't think so. You want to know what my problem is?

OTTO: Not especially.

KATE: I track down leads about some twelve-year-old's stolen Raleigh. I cover the grand openings of, let's see, bingo halls, electrolysis clinics, Weight Watchers. You name it, Murphy, I'm there. I'm hot. Mrs fucking Esposito's blender disappears: Kate's got a few inches in Community Corner for it. No problem not a problem hey I'm smiling see me smile see me take a photo of this new-born or that blue ribbon Alsatian no problem I'm happy I'm there and I WAS A COLUMNIST GOD-DAMNIT.

OTTO: Displays of excessive emotion bore me, Miss Buck.

KATE: I'm being watched by a person who lives in another country.

OTTO: Which country?

KATE: I don't know. Another one. Does it matter?

OTTO: I should think it matters a great deal. Canada is relatively nearby. England, on the other hand, is not.

KATE: England. Why do you say England?

**Lights up on SUZY. She works out on an exercise bike while writing a letter.**

OTTO: An obsession with unanswerable questions is the first sign of insanity. Concern yourself with easy answers. Find Lester Marquette and you will have the story of your life.

**OTTO exits. Music in: 'Native New Yorker' (Odyssey). KATE's been listening to this tune on her Walkman. She listens to the song seriously for a moment, then removes a letter from her bag and reads it as she bops along to the music.**

SUZY (*plugging away on the bicycle*): Dear Kate Buck. My advert, which ought to have run in *Astrology Monthly*, mistakenly ran in *Looking for Love*, a publication I am not familiar with. My life is a bit of a mess just at the moment so I'm not surprised by odd occurrences. I think it has something to do with the upcoming solar eclipse and also my Mars is in Scorpio, which explains a great deal. But enough about me. Yes, I am interested in holistic healing, crystals, natural childbirth, macrobiotics and the lot, but I am fairly certain that I'm not a lesbian. I mean, I'm always receptive to new experiences. An astrologer has to be. But I have to admit I enjoy a good rogering every once in a while and therefore I feel your letters, however sensitive and entertaining, are quite missing their mark. I'm sorry, but since I've rarely been outside of London, I don't see how I could have been born in New York City. And as your dream date is a native New Yorker, I'm afraid that leaves me out. One of my ex-boyfriends lives somewhere near New York City, and he once sent me a miniature Statue of Liberty. But that's as close as I got, since he stopped writing to me shortly afterwards. Though I do thank you for the cassette. I have fond memories of dancing with my gay friend, Martin, to that song in the late seventies. Good luck in your search and I'd appreciate your not writing to me again. Unless, of course, you'd like me to prepare your chart. I'm sure we could agree on a rate. Sincerely, Suzy Bradfield.

**Lights down on SUZY. KATE folds up the letter carefully, kisses it, puts it back in her bag. She removes her 9mm automatic pistol from the bag and once again begins the ritual of cleaning it. Music out.**
**Shift focus to AVA and CALVIN on a street in Arlington, Virginia. AVA consults a map.**

CALVIN: We should have headed west, Ava Coo.

AVA: Look. I got sick of you back in Pennsylvania in that that – what the hell was that loony tunes town you dragged me through –

CALVIN: It was an Amish village.

AVA: Yeah, well, they were fucking out to lunch.

CALVIN: I'm interested in the way they live.

AVA: What's to be interested in? They don't have zippers. What kind of people don't have zippers? I'll tell you, Calvin. Wackos. That's who.

CALVIN: They do just as well with buttons, Ava Coo.

AVA: I'm gonna shove a button up your ass if you don't stop calling me Ava Coo like I'm some kind of . . . bug. Ava. A-V-A. Get it?

CALVIN: Yours is a name that begs to be heard in its entirety. Like a Beethoven piano sonata.

AVA: Oh boy. Listen to me Liberace: THIS IS MY TRIP. Okay? It's my trip, it's my car, it's my map and we go where I say we go. And we are going south. As soon as I figure out why my friggin' car won't start.

CALVIN: It's not your car any more.

AVA: Just . . . why do you do that? Huh? Never got anything good to say. Always bringing me down. DownDOWNDOWN.

CALVIN: And actually, it's my map.

AVA: I'm gonna put my fist through your ugly fat face if you don't SHUT UP about it already. I swear to God those fruitcake Amish put some kind of fucking hex on me and my car.

CALVIN: You shouldn't blame others for your own misfortune.

AVA: You know, you really ought to do some evangelising 'cause you'd make a fortune with this thine neighbour thyself thou holy shit. (*A beat.*) I shouldn't have laughed at that Amish kid's pants. I knew they were into that voodoo hoodoo crap. Shitshit. Where the hell are we?

CALVIN: Arlington, Virginia. President Kennedy's buried here. Would you like to see his grave?

AVA: Fuck off.

CALVIN: Respect history and it will respect you.

AVA: You're unbelievable. It's like you drop a coin in your mouth and some stupid saying comes out your ass.

CALVIN: His grave has an eternal flame. I'd like to see it.

AVA: Listen. I wasn't even born when Kennedy, you know, rest in peace and all that shit, and my mother didn't vote for him. So go yourself. Bye-bye.

CALVIN: The very thought of an eternal flame fills my heart with an inexplicable longing. Why don't you feel it?

AVA: You're really freaking me out, Calvin. Why don't you take the car, okay, take the car and do . . . whatever you gotta do with it. I'll hitch.

CALVIN: I can't leave you.

AVA: Sure you can. I'm like a doormat. People coming and going, breaking and entering, the whole time.

CALVIN: I'm sorry, but I'm meant to be with you.

AVA: I'm pretty sure I was meant to be with Paul Newman, but I'm not so.

CALVIN: My face isn't fat. And I'm not ugly. At least I don't think I am. Am I?

AVA: What — okay, no. You're not ugly. I'm sorry.

CALVIN: What about my face? Is it fat? Do you really think it's fat?

AVA: I don't — it's just an expression. Like when you're mad at somebody you say, you know, you say, fuck you, you fat face bastard. Like that.

CALVIN: A figure of speech.

AVA: Yeah. Whatever. (*Beat.*) How many phone books can we go through in how many hick towns looking for some dive that probably doesn't exist?

CALVIN: It exists.

AVA: How do you know? How do you know that Mink guy wasn't pulling my pud? People always pull my pud. I have that kind of face.

CALVIN: You're beautiful.

AVA: All right all right. Don't start up again. I'm warning you.

**KATE enters. She listens to her Walkman intently and dangles the pistol nonchalantly. She's in a world only she understands and therefore doesn't notice AVA and CALVIN.**

AVA: Ohmygod I've read about this kind of right-wing southern lunatic with a gun. Ohmygod we're gonna die.

CALVIN: She's just . . . walking. Thinking. Relax.

AVA: She's probably on her way to a . . . a post office or or . . . a MacDonald's — yeah — some fast food joint where she's gonna, I don't know, burn her bra and shoot till she ain't got any fingers left. Get me out of here, Calvin. Weirdos stick to me like I'm flypaper. I'm serious.

**CALVIN approaches KATE. AVA drops to her knees. Crosses herself every which way.**

AVA: Now I lay me down to sleep . . . oh fuck that's not right. What is it? WHAT IS THE FUCKING PRAYER.

**CALVIN puts his hand on KATE's shoulder. She turns to him. A beat. She removes her headphones, puts them in her purse.**

KATE: You're from England, aren't you?

CALVIN: I am.

KATE: I knew that.

CALVIN: I'm impressed.

KATE: I was a Pulitzer prize-winning columnist for the *Philadelphia Inquirer*.

CALVIN: I'm a repossessions man. Depressing, but it's a living.

KATE (*refers to* AVA): Is your friend hurt?

CALVIN: She's praying.

KATE: I like spiritual women.

CALVIN: Do you have a Yellow Pages?

KATE: Yes I do.

CALVIN: Do you know anything about cars?

KATE: What make?

CALVIN: Chevy Nova. 1974.

KATE: That's the same as mine. What colour?

**A beat, before they answer simultaneously.**

KATE and CALVIN: Yellow.

CALVIN: It's my friend's car. Well, I'm in the process of repossessing it, but . . . she's got a night-club engagement she's got to get to in the meantime. (*Refers to the gun.*) Are you afraid of something?

KATE: Everything. (*Refers to his hand on her shoulder.*) You have a very comforting touch.

CALVIN: Thank you. I took a massage class on Long Island.

KATE: New York. You're here from New York?

CALVIN: That's right.

KATE: Is your friend from New York?

CALVIN: Born and bred.

KATE: Really.

CALVIN: I feel I'm meant to marry her. But something tells me she doesn't want it to work out.

KATE: Really.

**KATE gently removes CALVIN's hand from her shoulder. She approaches AVA, who's been silently praying to herself, eyes shut tight against the threat of potential violence. KATE taps AVA with the pistol.**

AVA (*with great speed, as if she's been holding this in all the while*): I'm just as uncomfortable with blacks Jews democrats shriners Irish and you know whatever as you are please don't kill me I'm on the verge of a spectacular singing career if only I could find the Tumbleweed Junction.

KATE: I'm a journalist. I don't take sides.

AVA (*she opens her eyes*): Oh. Thankyougod. (*Refers to the gun*). Is it dangerous around here?

KATE: No. Somebody's watching me, though. What's your name?

AVA: Ava. Ava Coo.

KATE: Ava Coo. Ava Coo. Hmmm.

AVA: Fuck me, not another one who has a thing about my name.

KATE: Are you going out with anybody?

AVA: Oh sure. Maybe. Yeah . . . well. Not really. No. Definitely not.

KATE (*refers to the pistol*): I'll put this away now.

**She does. She holds out her hand to AVA. A beat, before AVA takes KATE's hand. KATE lifts AVA to her feet.**

KATE: I understand you have car trouble.
AVA: You ever hear of a club called Tumbleweed Junction?
KATE: Come home with me and we'll discuss it.

**Music in: 'Follow Me' (Amanda Lear).**

# joe penhall
## from *Some Voices*

Joe Penhall's plays include *Wild Turkey* (Old Red Lion, 1993),
*Some Voices* (Royal Court Theatre Upstairs, 1994) and *Pale
Horse* (Royal Court Theatre Upstairs, 1995). He is currently
Thames Television writer-in-residence at the Royal National
Theatre.

critical mass

**PETE's flat. Morning. PETE is sitting at a kitchen table, RAY enters carrying a four-pack of beer and wearing a long old coat. He looks dishevelled, sleepless. They look at each other.**

RAY: All right, Pete?

PETE: Yeh I'm all right, you all right?

RAY: Yeh.

PETE: Where you been?

RAY: Oh here and there.

PETE: Well where? What's the matter – couldn't you sleep?

RAY: It's the room you gave me. The walls keep moving. It's shrinking.

PETE: What d'you mean shrinking? D'you have a nightmare?

RAY: I told you. It's getting smaller. It's a nice place, Pete, but it's definitely getting smaller.

PETE: Don't be daft. Smaller?

RAY: Where's the railway line? It was out there a minute ago.

PETE (*indicating beers*): What's this?

RAY: D'you know I always like to know where the railway line is. Increases my sense of mobility.

PETE: Where'd you get 'em?

RAY: When does the train come?

PETE: Never mind when the train comes. Where d'you get those?

RAY: I found 'em.

PETE: Where did you find 'em?'

RAY: An old man gave 'em to me.

PETE: What old man?

RAY: This old fella down by the canal. I don't know his name. I was watching the sunrise and there were lots of 'em all asleep.

PETE: What have you done?

RAY: It's all different now. Most of it's wasteland but on some they planted trees, plant boxes, little pathways.

PETE: And this fella just gave you his beers, just like that.

RAY: I was thirsty.

PETE: You didn't do anything, did you?

RAY: No. You want one?

**PETE pulls out a little phial of capsules from his pocket, shakes it.**

PETE: Just hand 'em over. Have some breakfast and take one of these.

RAY: Is it just me or are things not the same colour any more?

PETE: What d'you mean?

RAY: Green things. Green things aren't the same any more, much more faded. Yellow's not the same any more neither. And then there's the sun which is more . . . white. Silver. It's either too bright or else not even there. And the sky.

PETE: Yeh all right, Ray . . .

RAY: Look at the sky, Pete. It's not the same. It's not even a proper blue any more. Everything is different.

PETE: Ray.

**PETE pushes the phial towards RAY.**

RAY: No thanks.

PETE: You have to, Ray, you know you do.

RAY: I'm not taking any more of that stuff. It addles my brain. Affects my judgment.

**RAY swigs on a beer and grins at PETE who holds out his hand for the beer.**

PETE: Give it to me.

RAY: You know what those are, Pete?

PETE: I know what they are and I know you need 'em.

RAY: Horse tranquillisers. Major knockout drops.

PETE: Just take a couple.

RAY: Chlorpromazine. Like Lithium times ten. Or a smack on the head with a claw-hammer, if you know what that's like. Hardly the elixir of life.

PETE: Listen –

RAY: I'm not listening.

PETE: If this stuff is going to keep you out of that place and stop you doing stupid things then you have to take 'em.

RAY: I don't want to.

PETE: That's not the point.

RAY: Well what is the point?

**Pause.**

RAY: Have a beer with me, Pete. Let's sit down and talk about old times together.

PETE: We will, Ray, but first you have to do this. If this is going to work, you have show willing.

RAY: Bollocks. Since when did willing get anyone anywhere? Eh? Eh Pete?

**Pause.**

RAY: Thanks for picking me up yesterday.

PETE: It was a pleasure.

RAY: No I mean it. When you came to the gate in the car and you got out and opened the boot for my bags it was . . . it was a good feeling. I mean I really had that, that leaving feeling. That feeling. That feeling of leaving . . . and arriving.

PETE: Good.

RAY: Remember all those times when you were either picking me up from somewhere or dropping me off? Taking me to the train. Meeting me off the coach. Remember the time I got lost in Scotland? Perth. Took myself off and got arseholed with the old men of Perth for three weeks.

PETE: Yeh, it was very clever.

RAY: And remember the time I got lost in Wales?

PETE: It's difficult to forget, Ray.

RAY: Tenby. Got myself arseholed with the young people of Tenby for three weeks. All rock shops and little pubs done up to look like barns and little barns done up to look like pubs.

PETE: Give us the beers will you.

RAY: Leaving and arriving, Pete, that's what I was doing. Following a pattern established over years which —

PETE: The beers, Ray.

RAY: Because I'm a travelling man.

PETE: Ray.

RAY: Swap.

PETE (confused): No, no swaps. I mean yes, swap.

**PETE holds out the pills, RAY holds out the beers, withdrawing them as PETE tries to grab them. Eventually PETE takes the four-pack and RAY takes the phial of pills. PETE stands, puts the beers out of reach.**

RAY: Hey, Pete.

PETE: Yes, Ray.

RAY: I'm sorry I never made the wedding.

**Pause.**

PETE: Well, you were tied up, weren't you.

RAY: I was going to be best man, wasn't I?

PETE: That's right, yeh.

RAY: I had a special little book and everything, all about what you do when you're a best man. The 'etiquette' of being a best man.

PETE: And what do you do?

RAY: I dunno. Never read it.

**Pause.**

RAY: And, and I'm sorry I never made the divorce neither.

PETE: You didn't miss much.

RAY: Quick, wasn't it?

PETE: Like lightning.

RAY: I mean it, Pete. I am sorry. You been growing into an old fart without me.

PETE: Well, you disappeared. Things change when you disappear.

RAY: That's what I was saying, Pete. Everything's changed. Even the . . . even the smells have changed.

PETE: Ray, listen . . .

RAY: Except for one. One smell hasn't changed.

PETE: Ray, please . . .

RAY: Remember when we was kids and we used to play in that old stream that runs underneath the brewery?

PETE: No.

RAY: Yes you do. We'd play with sticks having races. And sometimes the horses from the brewery came down and drank there. And sometimes dad came down and drank there and all, when he was working at the brewery. You remember that smell? That **mysterious** smell which we could never figure out what it was.

PETE: Horse shit.

RAY: Nah, it was a nice smell.

PETE: Ray, I've got to go to work.

RAY: I've figured out what it was. You want to know what it was. Pete? It was hops.

**Pause. They look at each other.**

PETE: I'm expecting deliveries. You going to go and see that woman today?

**RAY opens the phial and tosses a capsule in the air, catches it in his mouth like a peanut.**

RAY: What woman's that then?
PETE: The one they fixed you up with to sort out the thingie for your whatsit.
RAY: What whatsit?
PETE: After-sales service.

**RAY throws another capsule in the air, catches it in his mouth.**

RAY: You want one?
PETE: No thanks.
RAY: It'll calm you down.
PETE: When are you going?
RAY: I'm not going.
PETE: You're going, Ray.

**RAY shakes his head.**

PETE: Have a bath and get ready.
RAY: I didn't ask to be fixed up with any woman.
PETE: You gotta do it, Ray. The people said you gotta do it. She'll fix you up with that fella. He's supposed to be very good.
RAY: What fella?
PETE: The fella they recommended for the whatsit.
RAY (*exasperated*): What whatsit?!
PETE (*beat*): Observation. He's gonna help you now you're out.
RAY: Help me?
PETE: Watch you. See you don't get in any/trouble.
RAY: He's not gonna help me.
PETE: Yes he/is, Ray.
RAY: They're not here to help, these people.
PETE: They're here to –
RAY: They're here to investigate the mind.
PETE: Yes. **Your** mind.
RAY: For fun.
PETE: No, not for fun!

RAY: Because they find it interesting. They do.

PETE: Ray!

**Pause. PETE pulls out a ten-pound note from his pocket and hands it to RAY.**

RAY: What's this?

PETE: Money.

RAY: I thought we were going to talk.

PETE: Call me when you're finished. I'll give you directions, we'll talk.

RAY: I know where it is.

PETE: Corner of Askew and –

RAY: Yeh yeh yeh off you go.

**PETE hesitates, then puts on a jacket and exits. Pause. RAY tips his head back, spits the capsules one by one into the air and catches them in his hand. Puts them back in the bottle, stands, grabs the beers and exits.**

# paul godfrey
from *Fearquest*

Paul Godfrey was born in Exeter and is a playwright and director. His plays are: *Inventing a New Colour* (Bristol Old Vic/ Royal Court Theatre Upstairs), *A Bucket of Eels* (RSC Festival), *Once in a While the Odd Thing Happens* and *The Blue Ball* (both RNT Cottesloe) and *The Modern Husband* (ATC). *The Candidate*, after Flaubert, is due to be produced by the Royal Shakespeare Company in 1996. The scene which follows is work-in-progress from a new play for a large cast.

**CHICO, LEWIS and JEAN. JEAN talks aside.**

JEAN: When I wake
I have no fear
until I recall it.
Once I recall it
I bury it deep,
deep in my chest.
As I walk out
I am unaware
that I am carrying it,
I carry it carefully
to keep it safe
deep in my chest.
I mustn't be shaken
or jolted,
I walk out carefully
hoping I'll be safe.
(My fear weighs nothing
it isn't heavy
so I am not aware
of its weight!)
I think if I wasn't safe
if I were threatened
if something happened
it could be sharp,
it could cut me.
Like sharp glass
I carry it in me
and it will cut me,
if I am threatened,
if I am jolted,
when something happens.
I hope I can be careful,
careful enough
to keep it safe deep
in my chest
until I sleep.

**CHICO reads out loud.**

CHICO: Being attacked, planes, motorway driving, razors, the sea, absolute darkness, heights . . .

LEWIS (*to* JEAN): Where did you get this list?

JEAN: I asked him to ring and ask some friends to tell him three frightening things each.

LEWIS: Start again.

CHICO: Being attacked, planes, motorway driving, razors, the sea, absolute darkness, heights, spiders, cows, rats, life . . .

LEWIS: Life?

CHICO: Yes life. A friend of mine is frightened of life. Life itself. All life. Life, death, being inadequate, annihilation, maggots, bridges, exposure, going blind, income tax, snakes, pain and violence.

JEAN: No mention of nuclear war?

CHICO: No one's frightened of that any more.

LEWIS: What use is this strange catalogue?

JEAN: As good a starting point as any other.

LEWIS: I see. Add dentists then.

CHICO: Can I make a suggestion?
I'd like to categorise what we've got.
Arrange the different fears in groups.
Can we divide them all between internal or
external fears, for example?

JEAN: Why not real fears and imaginary fears?

LEWIS: Or frightening **things**, frightening **actions**
and frightening **situations**?

JEAN (*to* CHICO): Your idea. Let's try your categories first.

CHICO: Internal and external.

LEWIS: Is life 'internal' or 'external' then?

JEAN: Internal.

CHICO: External.

JEAN: The **experience** of life is internal.

CHICO: How can life be internal?

LEWIS: It's both external **and** internal, isn't it?

CHICO: OK. Let's try 'real' and 'imaginary' instead.
Life is real.

LEWIS: True. This is real, here, now.

JEAN: Annihilation is real.

CHICO: Imaginary surely.

JEAN: No. I've seen it.

CHICO: You won't be there when you're annihilated.

LEWIS: We shall all be annihilated.

She's right. It's real.

CHICO: Perhaps 'annihilation' is a situation?

LEWIS: Let's try 'things', 'actions' and 'situations'.

JEAN: Is income tax 'a thing', 'an action' or 'a situation'?

CHICO: Neither is it?

LEWIS: You've not paid any yet.

Income tax is a situation like annihilation is a situation.

JEAN (*reads*): Being attacked, planes, motorway driving, razors, the sea, absolute darkness, heights, spiders, cows, rats, life, death, being inadequate, annihilation, maggots, bridges, exposure, going blind, income tax, snakes, pain, violence and dentists.

LEWIS: Personally I would drop 'cows' and 'life'.

Cows are comic, life is unspecific.

CHICO: What about fear of animals?

Animals is a clear category isn't it?

LEWIS: Except for spiders, spiders are insects.

JEAN: I have a category.

I'd like to talk about the unknowable fears.

LEWIS: What are the unknowable fears?

JEAN: Most of the items on the list:

razors, darkness, motorway driving,

these are knowable fears

but death, annihilation, the end of the world

they are not.

CHICO: Are they fears if you're not frightened of them? Those things don't frighten me.

JEAN: What are you frightened of then?

CHICO: Nothing I know of.

(*Aside.*) When I came here I paid by cheque.

I produced my cheque book.

'Can I pay by cheque?' I asked.

The ticket-seller looked at me.

'A Jewish cheque book' he said.

'What?'

'Why is it a Jewish cheque book?'

I enquired.
'A cheque book without a pen' he said.
'Can you lend me a pen?' I asked.
'Isn't that a bit stupid?' he said.
'Why?'
I asked.
'To carry a cheque book without a pen' he replied.
Then when he gave me the ticket
before I turned to go
'I am Jewish'
I said.
JEAN: What are you frightened of then?
CHICO: Nothing I know of.
LEWIS: Got the right job then haven't you?
JEAN: So when you are faced with death
or the end of the world or annihilation
what will you feel?
CHICO: I don't know.
LEWIS: Fear defies the categories doesn't it?
JEAN (to CHICO): You've got a lot to learn.
CHICO: This is my first job.
JEAN: He gave me my first job,
once upon a time . . .
LEWIS: Let me admit something to you both.
I'm due to retire next year.
Within eighteen months we'll see the end of
this corporation.
I'm not exaggerating when I say
'These are the final days!'
All those years I edited the News
even when I had a free hand
I knew it wasn't the news itself,
whatever that might be?
For a long time I puzzled over it
until eventually I came to this idea,
take one familiar word
and try to find out what it means.
JEAN: You asked us to explore fear

but I'm not clear what you expect from us.
LEWIS: I want to call it
A PROGRAMME ABOUT FEAR
but the rest is up to you.
JEAN: If this was a story I'd be happier
then I'd know exactly what to do.
LEWIS: There isn't always a story.
I want you to report on life itself
I know you are the person to do this.
I chose you both deliberately.
CHICO: You want us to go and look
is there something you want us to find?
LEWIS: The word that unites us is fear.
This is the subject.
JEAN: Yes.
LEWIS (*to* JEAN): You recognise it.
You've seen enough.
JEAN: Elsewhere, never here
but perhaps that's why I am prepared to pursue this
because it gives me the chance
to take a look at it all, this, here,
my own home country?
LEWIS: Wherever I go, whatever I do
this is what I see:
Everything operates through fear.
JEAN: But what are we looking for exactly?
We need to know that.
LEWIS: What do you call it when you undertake
a search for something
but you don't know what it is?
CHICO: A wild goose chase?
JEAN: I am asking you to
lay the challenge before us explicitly and
then we can take it up.
LEWIS: I want you to find out what fear is.
CHICO: Who knows what fear is?
JEAN: Everyone knows what fear is.
LEWIS: But who can tell me?

JEAN: This is ludicrous
What is fear?
What is joy?
What is hate?
What is grief?
Everyone knows these feelings.
Everyone knows what the words mean,
but no one can tell you.
CHICO: What about people who are frightened?
They can tell us what fear is.
LEWIS (to JEAN): You don't accept the challenge?
JEAN: What do you think?
I've come halfway round the world
to work for you.
You know I accept.
CHICO: We can get a consensus
from the replies to the adverts.
We just have to go and ask . . .
LEWIS: I wonder about these advertisements.
Is that a valid approach?
Will anyone reply?
If a fear's a real fear
who wants to admit it?
JEAN: What else do you suggest then?
CHICO: I went to the public library to get some self-help books. But they
were all out on loan.
LEWIS: I have an idea.
Let's begin now.
Test something for yourselves.
I see fear everywhere.
I want you each to go
and take a walk in the street
look at what you see
and come back and tell me.
But don't question this.
Go now. Look.
JEAN: Why not?
I'm jet-lagged.

I need daylight.
CHICO: Perhaps it'll come to us?
Perhaps we needn't seek it out?
LEWIS: You have ten minutes.

**Exit JEAN and CHICO.**

LEWIS (*aside*): I have this fear
and it plagues me
and I don't know what I can do about it.

# nick ward

## from *The Present*

Nick Ward was born in Geelong, Australia in 1962. His work as
a writer-director includes *Eastwood* (Man in the Moon), *Apart
from George* (RNT Studio, Royal Court Theatre Upstairs and
tour), *The Strangeness of Others* (RNT Cottesloe) and two
feature films: *Dakota Road* and *Look Me in the Eye*. *The
Present* marked his return to live theatre after some years and
was premièred at the Bush Theatre in 1995.

**It is 1980. Eighteen-year-old** DANNY RULE **is backpacking round Australia at the time John Lennon dies. Claiming to be an English artist, Luke Murray, he sells fake landscapes to earn money. While doing this, he discovers that an old friend,** LIBBY, **who is a real artist, is living nearby.**

BECKY **and** LIBBY**'s place.** DANNY **is at the door.**

DANNY: My name's Luke . . . Danny Rule. I'm looking for Libby Meyer . . . Am I in the right place?

BECKY: How do you know Libby?

DANNY: I'm a close friend.

BECKY: Well, any friend of Libby's is a – what did you say your name was . . . ?

DANNY: Danny Rule.

BECKY: . . . friend of mine, Danny. Come in. She'll be back soon. Take a seat.

DANNY: Thanks.

**He does so. Silence.**

BECKY: Comfy?

DANNY: Thanks.

BECKY **lights a stick of incense.**

BECKY: Libby hasn't mentioned you.

DANNY: No? Any idea when she might get back?

BECKY: Presently. She's on her way back from Kalgoorlie.

DANNY: Aaah!

BECKY: You've been there?

DANNY: Briefly.

BECKY: So, that's where you met her?

DANNY: No, no, I knew her in England.

BECKY: '76?

DANNY: That's right.

BECKY: A very hot summer in England.

DANNY: That's right. How do you know that?

BECKY: Libby told me. She said it was like being in Australia. Funny that.

DANNY: What?

BECKY: That she should mention the weather, but not an extremely close friend who calls himself Danny Rule. It's a bit odd, if you ask me.

DANNY: Well, it's certainly surprising.

BECKY: So what did you think of Kalgoorlie? Did you go to the brothel?

DANNY: No. No. Actually I was staying in a place quite near Kalgoorlie, called . . . Kookynie. I loved it. It's an old ghost town. Really atmospheric. You know there are old cars, just sitting in the sand, untouched since the . . .

BECKY: . . . sand? You mean **earth**? We don't call it sand.

DANNY: Anyway, they really struck me. A kind of monument to the pioneering men of Australia.

BECKY: What about the women? What about the pioneering women of Australia?

DANNY: Men and women, that's what I meant to say.

BECKY: I don't think you did. I don't think it occurred to you to say 'women'. How do you think your omission leaves me feeling?

DANNY: I didn't mean to offend you.

BECKY: It leaves me feeling pretty fucking excluded, Danny.

**She lights a joint.**

DANNY: I'm sorry.

BECKY: What did you say you were doing in Kalgoorlie?

DANNY: Just having a look. Part of my trip.

BECKY: It's a pretty funny place to go for a holiday.

DANNY: Well, I had my sketch book with me.

BECKY: You're an artist? Libby won't like that.

DANNY: No, I wouldn't say I was an artist.

BECKY: You just said you were in Kalgoorlie with a sketch book. When was this?

DANNY: Oh, a few weeks ago.

BECKY: Libby was there then.

DANNY: I wish I'd known that.

BECKY: Were you alone?

DANNY: Yeah, I was feeling pretty down. My girlfriend had just dumped me.

BECKY: Good for her. You won't find many women choosing to be in Kalgoorlie. I expect you feel at home with all that maleness – brothels –

two up – miners – machinery. I expect you get off on what men have
done to this country.

DANNY: Oh, no, quite the reverse. I think it's tragic. They've raped it.

BECKY: I hate it when men use that word. Here do you want a smoke?

DANNY: No thanks, not for me.

BECKY: Go on. Be a devil. You might get more interesting.

DANNY: No, really, I ought to get going. Would you mind telling Libby
that I called . . . ?

BECKY (*interrupting*): She'll be back soon – any minute. Please don't go.
I'm a bit lonely actually.

**She smokes the joint, then passes it to** DANNY. BECKY **goes over to a tape-
deck.** DANNY **sits down on a sofa.** BECKY **selects a tape and puts it on. It's a
John Lennon compilation.**

DANNY: So what was Libby doing in Kalgoorlie?

BECKY: Fuck off, smart arse. (*Pause.*) I'm sorry. I'm really sorry, Danny.
I didn't mean that. I miss her, that's all.

DANNY: Don't mention it.

BECKY: How did you know to come here?

DANNY: I'm staying with a close friend of hers. He gave me the address.

BECKY: He?

DANNY: Michael.

BECKY: Michael?

DANNY: Yeah, do you know him?

BECKY: I know Michael alright. I hate that man.

DANNY: Oh.

BECKY: He's a fucking jumped-up parasite. The art world's full of them.

DANNY: That's interesting.

BECKY: Why is it interesting?

DANNY: I don't know.

BECKY: I hate small-talk.

DANNY: I'm sorry.

BECKY: Don't apologise.

**Pause.**

DANNY: So, what do you do?

BECKY: I'm old money. What about you?

DANNY: I'm a bit broke, actually.

BECKY: Oh, dear! Bad luck. I'm also a writer, and I look after Libby.

DANNY: What are you writing?

BECKY: A book.

DANNY: Oh.

**Pause.**

BECKY: It's about art and it's about women. I can't tell you any more.

DANNY: Sounds interesting, anyway.

BECKY: I may call it 'Conflicting Messages'. What do you think of the title?

DANNY: How do you feel about it?

BECKY: That's the right answer, Danny-boy. So, tell me more about you and Libby. In **England**.

**She sits on the arm of the sofa, facing him.**

DANNY: Oh, she was great. She taught me such a lot.

BECKY: What about?

DANNY: Everything, everything. She was great.

BECKY: How old were you?

DANNY: Fourteen.

BECKY: And what exactly did she teach you? Do you think I'm attractive?

DANNY: Very much so.

BECKY: Why?

DANNY: Well, you've got . . . um . . .

BECKY: Do you know how much I weighed when I was fourteen? Five stone. And there wasn't any Libby in my life, I can tell you. But, I'm alright now. Look. (*She caresses herself.*) Don't you think?

DANNY: You're lovely.

BECKY: I hate my father. So?

DANNY: So?

BECKY: I asked you what happened between you and Libby, in the summer of '76.

DANNY: It sounds stupid now, but she changed my life.

BECKY: There's something you ought to know about Libby, Danny.

DANNY: Is there?

BECKY: About that time. In England.

DANNY: What?

BECKY: It was a bad time for her.

DANNY: I thought she had a really nice time. She was staying with my family.

BECKY: Well, she didn't. It was a terrible time, which is why she's wiped most of it. I thought you ought to know.

DANNY: Thanks . . . I didn't catch your name.

BECKY: I'm Libby's flatmate. That'll do. Do you like John Lennon?

DANNY: I love him.

BECKY: Terrible to die like that. Two of the bullets went straight through him. He must have looked a real mess. The worst part was the policeman who drove him to the hospital, do you know what he asked him?

DANNY: No.

BECKY: 'Are you John Lennon?' John Lennon said he was, then he died. I mean fuck me. Poor Yoko . . . Oh, I see, you love John Lennon, but you hate Yoko Ono.

DANNY: I didn't say that.

BECKY: All men hate Yoko.

DANNY: I think that's a bit of a generalisation.

BECKY (*overlapping* DANNY): Because she's a strong woman, because she's an artist and because she isn't white.

DANNY (*overlapping* BECKY): Sure, if you call 'A hole to look at the sky through' art, I'll go along with you.

BECKY: Can you see my knickers?

DANNY: That's strong grass.

**He puts the joint out.**

BECKY: It's Moroccan hash. Can you?

DANNY: Yes.

BECKY: Do you like what you see? Pretty erotic isn't it? Looking up a strange woman's skirt. You're all eyes.

DANNY: It must be the hash.

BECKY: I'm a strong woman, Danny, but I'm being a very naughty girl, don't you think? Have you got a hard-on?

**From where she is sitting on the arm of the sofa, she very deliberately stretches one leg out and kicks him.**

BECKY: Ooo! Sorry, my foot slipped.

DANNY: Hey!

BECKY: I think Danny-boy's a bit out of his depth.

DANNY: You're really freaking me out.
BECKY: Great. (*She stands up.*) Wait a minute. Don't go away.

**She turns the music up. She starts to dance, very provocatively, she dances closer and closer to DANNY, eventually moving behind him, as she does so she suddenly hits him on the head.**

DANNY: Don't hit me.
BECKY: Why not?
DANNY: It's fucking irritating.
BECKY: Getting angry, eh? Makes you want to hit me back, eh? Go on then, give it a go, if you dare.

**She jumps on top of him, lunging at him sexually and hitting him wildly.**

DANNY: Please stop. Please. This is really freaking me out.

**He escapes. She is up like a flash and stands in front of him, blocking his way.**

BECKY: I know.
DANNY: How do you know?
BECKY: Because I can see things.

**She pushes him back on to the sofa and kisses him violently.**

BECKY: Where are you going, Danny-boy?
DANNY: I'm going.
BECKY: Please don't go, Danny, I can't stand it. People are always going.

**Danny struggles. BECKY locks her legs around him. Confusion: she is thrusting herself against him. Her hands around his throat. As DANNY attempts to enter her she starts to strangle him. He can't breathe. He panics – attempting to pull her hands away from his throat. He succeeds, but their bodies are locked together – out of control. BECKY seems to go into some kind of spasm. It is a few moments before DANNY realises that she isn't moving. Her hands limply around her own throat. DANNY gets up slowly. He leaves as the John Lennon track swells.**

# philip ridley
## from *The Fastest Clock in the Universe*

Philip Ridley is a painter, novelist, filmmaker and playwright.
He was born in the East End of London, where he still lives
and works. He is the winner of numerous awards including a
unique double of *Evening Standard* Awards for Most
Promising Newcomer to British Film and Most Promising
Playwright (for *The Fastest Clock in the Universe*). His other
stage plays include *The Pitchfork Disney* (Bush Theatre, 1991)
and *Ghost From a Perfect Place* (Hampstead Theatre, 1994).
He wrote the screenplay for *The Krays* (1990) and has written
and directed two feature films, *The Reflecting Skin* (1990) and
*The Passion of Darkly Noon* (1995).

**A dilapidated room above an abandoned factory in the East End of London. Many large cracks in walls. Table, hard-backed chairs, sofa, cupboard, sideboard, window aglow with setting sunlight, fridge, sink, gas cooker, mirror. The main feature, however, is birds: stuffed birds, china birds, paintings of birds, etc., giving the room an atmosphere somewhere between museum and aviary. Two doors: the first leading to bedroom, the second to a corridor outside.**

COUGAR GLASS **is a young-looking thirty-year-old, sun-tanned, well-built, hair jet black and roughly styled in a quiff. He is wearing a white T-shirt, faded denim jeans and dark glasses.** CAPTAIN TOCK **is forty-two years old, pale, slightly built and balding. He is wearing a button-up white shirt (without tie) and a black suit. They are making last-minute preparations for a party celebrating** COUGAR's **nineteenth birthday, to which he has invited one very special guest.**

**Slowly** CAPTAIN **goes over to** COUGAR.
**They spread some magazines on floor and start sorting through them.**

CAPTAIN: What does Foxtrot like?

COUGAR: Women with women.

CAPTAIN: Lesbians.

COUGAR: The very same. Find me a good one, Captain. With lots of pictures. Christ Almighty! Some of these magazines go back to when I was twelve. That's how old I was when I got my first magazine. Me and my best friend stole it. We went to the block of flats where my friend lived and rushed up to the roof. We sat amongst the television aerials and looked at the photographs. I had an erection so hard it hurt. I persuaded my friend to get his cock out. I got mine out too. We played with each other. And then . . . then I got this feeling somewhere in my gut. Like a tiny explosion. And I came. It was my first ejaculation. I never dreamed a body could feel something like that. Christ Almighty! I'll never forget it. Sitting up there, amongst all those television aerials. Somehow, I felt as if I was part of an electric current. Every nerve in my body was transmitting particles of sex. My brain sparkled, my hair stood on end, blood simmered. I imagined myself glowing. A halo of lust buzzing round me. The first real moment of my life.

**Long pause.**

CAPTAIN **hands** COUGAR **magazine.**

CAPTAIN: Lesbians.

**COUGAR looks at magazine.**

COUGAR: Perfect.

**COUGAR goes to sofa.**

COUGAR: Put the magazines away, Captain.

**COUGAR hides magazine under sofa.**
**CAPTAIN starts to put magazines back in cupboard.**
**COUGAR practises sitting on sofa and reaching below to produce magazine in one swift movement.**
**CAPTAIN begins flicking through a magazine.**

CAPTAIN: I don't know what it is about the sight of skin that makes me weep.

**COUGAR looks at CAPTAIN.**
**Pause.**

COUGAR: Come on, slowcoach. We've got to get things ready.
CAPTAIN: Oh . . . yes. Of course.

**CAPTAIN puts remaining magazines in cupboard.**

COUGAR: Now, you know what to do, don't you, Captain?
CAPTAIN: Same as all the other parties, I suppose.
COUGAR: We'll let him in.
CAPTAIN: I know, Cougar. I know.
COUGAR: Have a few drinks.
CAPTAIN: That's why I bought the vodka.
COUGAR: Tell him how popular I am.
CAPTAIN: Thousands of girlfriends.
COUGAR: They follow me everywhere.
CAPTAIN: Like flies.
COUGAR: And all the time you're?
CAPTAIN: Pouring vodka.
COUGAR: Not too much. Don't want him to pass out.
CAPTAIN: Just tipsy.
COUGAR: Then I'll give you the signal to leave.
CAPTAIN: And I'll go. Farewell, Foxtrot Darling.

COUGAR: And the signal is?

CAPTAIN: What?

COUGAR: What's the signal for you to leave the party?

CAPTAIN: Good Lord! What is this? A test now?

COUGAR: Just tell me, Captain. I don't want any blunders tonight.

**Pause.**

CAPTAIN: You'll say, 'Isn't it time for your meeting, Captain?'

COUGAR: And you'll say?

CAPTAIN: 'Good Lord, yes, Cougar! Thank you for reminding me!'

COUGAR: And you'll disappear.

CAPTAIN: I'll have to walk the streets again, I suppose.

COUGAR: By the time you get back, he'll be gone.

CAPTAIN: And you'll never want to see him again.

COUGAR: Why would I want to see him again?

**CAPTAIN stares at COUGAR.**

**Pause.**

CAPTAIN (*softly*): Oh, Cougar.

**Pause.**

COUGAR: I haven't told you how I met him yet. And you've got to know, Captain. There's an extra bit this time.

CAPTAIN: What extra bit?

COUGAR: A sort of trap.

**CAPTAIN starts putting knives, forks, plates, glasses etc. on table.**

CAPTAIN: Good Lord! What now?

COUGAR: Listen. I was sunbathing in the park when . . . there he was. Walking very fast and holding some flowers. I was going to follow him then, but I couldn't get my boots on quick enough. You would have laughed.

**Pause.**

COUGAR: The next day I saw him again. Walking just as fast as before and holding some more flowers. But, again, I didn't get my boots on in time. So the following day, guess what I did?

**Pause.**

COUGAR: I didn't take my boots off! Good thinking, eh, Captain? This time, when I saw him, I was ready. I followed him. I really liked the way he walked. And then . . . then I saw where he was heading. The hospital. That's what the flowers were for. He was visiting someone sick. So I followed him into the hospital.

CAPTAIN: But you hate hospitals.

COUGAR: Shows you how much I wanted him. He went into a ward. I was going to follow him in there too, but a nurse stopped me. So I waited outside. But he was with a girl. She was clutching his arm. His girl-friend, I thought. I wanted to smash her fucking face in.

CAPTAIN: Temper, temper.

COUGAR: I couldn't help it, Captain. He was so perfect. She didn't deserve him. And that night I couldn't stop thinking about him. He was driving me mad. Oh, the table's coming along nicely, Captain.

CAPTAIN: I'm doing my best. So you went back to the hospital?

COUGAR: The very next day. I waited outside the ward. He turned up with some flowers and went inside. But this time he came out alone.

CAPTAIN: Your moment to pounce.

COUGAR: Exactly.

CAPTAIN: So who was he visiting?

COUGAR: His dying brother.

CAPTAIN: What was he dying of?

COUGAR: Oh, something terminal. And the girl, Captain – that floozie – she was his brother's girl-friend, not his. And then a plan started taking shape in my brain. The perfect trap.

**CAPTAIN has finished setting the table.**

CAPTAIN: There! All finished!

COUGAR: Sit down, Captain.

CAPTAIN: How does it look?

COUGAR: Fine. Just sit down.

CAPTAIN: You could show a little appreciation.

COUGAR: I said it looks fucking fine. What more do you want? A medal? Now just sit down.

**Pause. CAPTAIN sits.**

COUGAR: I've got to tell you about the trap.

**Pause.**

CAPTAIN: So? What was it?

**Pause.**

COUGAR: Savannah Glass.
CAPTAIN: Savannah Glass?
COUGAR: My wife.
CAPTAIN: Your what?
COUGAR: My dying wife. My wife who was in the same hospital as his dying brother.
CAPTAIN: Oh, no, Cougar.
COUGAR: Why shouldn't I have a wife?
CAPTAIN: I know you're not exactly the milk of human kindness, but not even you can be so cruel.
COUGAR: Don't make a song and dance out of it.
CAPTAIN: To play with someone's feelings like that. To manipulate them so callously.
COUGAR: But it's such a perfect lie, Captain. You see, it meant I didn't have to meet the dying brother's floozie either. I simply said I was too upset to meet other girls. Oh, come on. Credit where credit's due.
CAPTAIN: It's toying with someone's grief! To simply invent a wife in order to . . .
COUGAR (interrupting): I comforted him, Captain! Put my arm round him. Said I understood when he needed someone to understand. We suffered together. Sometimes he cried when I held him. Have you any idea what a buzz that is? And guess what, Captain. His brother and my wife -- what a coincidence! – they died on the same day.

CAPTAIN **stands.**

CAPTAIN: I won't be part of it.
COUGAR: You're already part of it!
CAPTAIN: I'm not. I'll go before Foxtrot gets here. It's too much, Cougar. Even for you. It's too heartless.
COUGAR: I thought you'd like it.
CAPTAIN: It's diabolical!
COUGAR: Spoil-sport!

CAPTAIN: Cannibal!

COUGAR: Cannibal!?

CAPTAIN: Yes! Cannibal!

COUGAR: Christ Almighty! The words you come up with.

CAPTAIN: To treat the boy like that . . .

COUGAR (*interrupting*): He's not a boy. He's a man.

CAPTAIN: How old is he?

COUGAR: Sixteen.

CAPTAIN: He's a boy!

COUGAR: He's a man. He can get married! He can have kids. He's a man for fuck's sake.

CAPTAIN: He's a boy and you've used him abominably.

COUGAR: I gave him what he wanted. A new big brother with a shoulder to cry on. So don't get all righteous with me. We're all as bad as each other. All hungry little cannibals at our own cannibal party. So fuck the milk of human kindness and welcome to the abbatoir!

# harwant bains

## from *Indian Summer*

Harwant Bains is the author of: *The Fighting Kite* (Theatre Royal, Stratford East), *Blood* (Royal Court Theatre Upstairs) and, for television, the prize-winning *Wild West* (Channel 4) and *Two Oranges and a Mango* (BBC). *Indian Summer* was commissioned by the Royal National Theatre Education Department as part of BT National Connections 1995.

KULWANT **is around ten years old. He has been taken to India by his mother after she had a row with his father. His friend** TITOO **is aged about fourteen,** NITA **eleven and her** BROTHER **six.**

### *A Holy Man on the Street*

KULWANT, TITOO, NITA **and her** BROTHER **walk along the narrow streets,** KULWANT **is clutching a new kite.**
**A beggar sits resting by the side of the street. He is dressed in the style of a holy man, and has a sword through his mouth.** KULWANT **stops short and stares at the** HOLY MAN **– the man turns and looks at him.**

TITOO: Come on.
KULWANT: He's got a big sword through his mouth.
TITOO: Yes. Come on.

**Beat.**

KULWANT: Why?
TITOO: Ask him.

KULWANT **approaches the man cautiously. He stands near to him for a moment.**

KULWANT: Excuse me. Why have you got that sword through your mouth? Doesn't it hurt?

**The** HOLY MAN **mumbles an incomprehensible reply.**

KULWANT (*to* TITOO): He can't speak either.
TITOO: That's not surprising.
KULWANT: Shall we take him to the hospital?
TITOO: Why?
KULWANT: A doctor could take out the sword. He's not bleeding.
TITOO: He doesn't want the sword taken out. He's a holy man.
KULWANT (*to the* HOLY MAN): Shall we take you to the hospital?

**The** HOLY MAN **shakes his head vigorously.**

KULWANT: Are you a holy man?

**The** HOLY MAN **nods his head.**

KULWANT: Do you talk to God?

**The HOLY MAN nods again.**

KULWANT: What do you say?

**The HOLY MAN looks baffled. He shrugs.**

TITOO: You never seen one of these types before?
KULWANT: No. I've seen lots of people without arms or legs.
NITA: You shouldn't talk to him any more.
KULWANT: Why not?
NITA: He might get angry and put the evil eye on us.
TITOO: You talk like your mother.
NITA: Things like that are true.

**KULWANT is looking at the HOLY MAN again.**

KULWANT: Shall I give him some money?
TITOO: What you scared of?
NITA: Yes, give him some – he won't get angry then.
TITOO: People like you should go back to the villages where you belong.
He can't do nothing to us.
NITA: How do you know?
TITOO: I'm not scared of him! Are you, Kulwant – are you scared?
KULWANT: Um, no . . .
TITOO: That's 'cause we're not bumpkins like Nita. You know what I'm
gonna do? – I'm gonna go and live in England so I can get away from all
the bumpkins in this town.
NITA (*pulling at* KULWANT's *shirt*): Let's go and fly the kite – come on.
TITOO: You still think I'm scared.
NITA: I don't want to talk to someone with the evil eye on them.
TITOO: What evil eye?

**He turns on the HOLY MAN.**

TITOO: You gonna put the evil eye on me, you old codger?

**The HOLY MAN makes no response.**

TITOO: Are you?

**The HOLY MAN just stares at TITOO. Suddenly furious, TITOO grabs the sword
at both ends and shakes the HOLY MAN's head from side to side, finally
pushing him back on the ground and standing over him. NITA has started**

**to cry – she is holding on to both** KULWANT **and her** BROTHER. **The** HOLY MAN
**holds his hands out in front of his face, he is moaning gently.**
**Pause.**

KULWANT: Shall we take out the sword?
NITA: No!
TITOO: Yeah – you take out the sword.

KULWANT **steps forward. He kneels down by the** HOLY MAN's **side.**

KULWANT: Will it hurt you if I take it out?

**The** HOLY MAN **stares at him in fear.**

KULWANT: I'll do it gently.

**He holds the scabbard.**

KULWANT: Tell me if it hurts.

**He starts to pull on the sword.** TITOO **looks disinterested and goes and sits
a few feet away. Despite their fear,** NITA **and her** BROTHER **move in closer to
watch.** KULWANT **turns around holding up the sword. The** HOLY MAN
**continues moaning softly behind them.** KULWANT **looks at** TITOO
**triumphantly.**

TITOO: You going to keep it?

KULWANT **nods.**

TITOO: Why don't you get rid of that hat? Tell your mother the wind
blew it away.

KULWANT **takes off the hat.**

NITA: Can I have it?
KULWANT: She'll see you wearing it.

**Beat.**

KULWANT: It doesn't matter. Tell her you found it somewhere.

**He puts it on her head.**

NITA: Is it a hat from England?
KULWANT: Yes.

**Beat.**

KULWANT: We bought it from a place next to the sea.

NITA: Is it a sea hat?

KULWANT: Yes.

NITA (*to her* BROTHER): It's a real English sea hat!

**KULWANT goes and sits next to TITOO.**

KULWANT: Why are all the houses around here red?

TITOO: It's the old Moslem district. This is where they all used to live.

KULWANT (*looking around*): They've got lovely patterns on the walls. Where did they go?

TITOO: Who?

KULWANT: The Moslems.

TITOO: A lot of them got killed here. They had their heads chopped off. Their blood covered these streets all over. My grandad used to tell us about it. A few got away and went to Pakistan.

**Beat.**

KULWANT: Who killed them?

TITOO: People did.

KULWANT: Why?

TITOO: 'Cause they were Moslems. It was when the British cut up the Punjab so the Moslems could have their own country.

**Beat.**

KULWANT: There might be ghosts here at night.

**Short pause.**

TITOO: Yeah, you never know. Come on, there's a good breeze going now – let's get that kite up.

**They get up and walk off, leaving the HOLY MAN still lying moaning by the side of the street.**

### *At the Stall Eating Tutti-Frutti*

**A small open-fronted stall which sells cigarettes, soft drinks, tea, snacks**

**and ice cream. A variety of people are standing around drinking tea,
eating and chatting. TITOO stands smoking a cigarette and joking with the
stallholder. The HOLY MAN sits to one side watching the comings and
goings.**
**KULWANT enters; he is carrying the sword he took from the HOLY MAN.**

TITOO: Hey Kulwant! You still got the sword – I thought your mother
would have taken it. (*To the* STALLHOLDER.) Have you met the boy from
London?
STALLHOLDER: London eh? (*Smiling.*) Which part of India is that in?
TITOO: You see these village types, Kulwant, they still think the earth is
flat!
STALLHOLDER: What shape do **you** think it is then, Professor?
KULWANT: Have you got any ice cream?
STALLHOLDER: The best ice cream in all India, sahib!
KULWANT: Have you got vanilla?
STALLHOLDER: Vanilla?
TITOO: He only has one flavour – tutti-frutti.
KULWANT: Is that all?

**Beat.**

KULWANT: I'll have that then.
STALLHOLDER (*putting the ice cream into a cone and handing it to*
KULWANT): Best tutti-frutti you'll ever taste!

**KULWANT makes to hand him some money.**

STALLHOLDER: Free to you, sahib!
TITOO: What did your mum think of the sword?
KULWANT: Nothing. I hid it.
TITOO: You going to use it? You going to chop off some bugger's head
with it?
KULWANT: I might do.
STALLHOLDER: How's the tutti-frutti, sahib? Tasty tasty eh?
KULWANT: It's nice.
STALLHOLDER: Nicey nicey eh?
TITOO: Anyone give you trouble, just swipe off his head with one stroke.
Then pick up the head, look the bloke in the eye and tell him, 'That'll
teach you to mess with a boy from London.'

KULWANT: He'd be dead by then.

TITOO: No he wouldn't, I've seen it for myself.

KULWANT: What?

TITOO: We had a bloke here in the market – just up over there. Fell off his bicycle and got his head cut clean off by the wheel of a truck – (*To the* STALLHOLDER.) you remember that, Ramchand?

STALLHOLDER: Last July it was.

TITOO: Some joker went and picked up the head. There was a big crowd there in seconds. We all saw the face. I swear to you that head was blinking, his eyes were moving around looking at us all – he looked surprised, kind of.

STALLHOLDER: His lips moved –

TITOO: – That's right! His lips moved too. Must have been like that for a couple of minutes, this head looking around at all of us, and us just staring back. Some bloke even went over and had a word with it.

KULWANT: What did he say?

TITOO: He said, 'Bad luck, old boy.' He reckons the head raised its eyebrows, kind of like a shrug saying, 'Well, that's life.' The police came and carried the head off to the bloke's house for the wife to identify.

**Beat.**

KULWANT (*touching the blade*): I don't think this is sharp enough to cut off anyone's head.

TITOO: That's easy to fix.

**Beat. KULWANT notices the HOLY MAN staring longingly at his sword. He walks over to him.**

KULWANT: Would you like an ice cream?

**Silence.**

KULWANT: It's nice, I'll buy you one if you like.

**The HOLY MAN looks sadly down at the ground.**

KULWANT (*to* TITOO): He doesn't talk.

TITOO: Some of these holy types are like that. They take all sorts of secret vows.

KULWANT (*to the* STALLHOLDER): Could I have another one please? I'll pay this time.

**The STALLHOLDER makes another cone.**

STALLHOLDER: No need for money, sahib, this one is for God.

**He hands the cone to KULWANT who takes it and offers it to the HOLY MAN.**

KULWANT: It's tutti-frutti.

**The HOLY MAN hesitates for a moment, then reaches out and takes the cone. KULWANT watches him as he eats.**

KULWANT: Do you like it?

**The HOLY MAN nods.**

STALLHOLDER: You will certainly have a long and happy life.
KULWANT: Why?
STALLHOLDER: Because you have made an offering to a man of God.
TITOO: If he's a 'man of God', I must be the President of India!
KULWANT: Maybe he really is.

**Beat.**

KULWANT: Would you like your sword back?

**The HOLY MAN looks at the sword.**

KULWANT: Would you like it back?

**Beat.**

KULWANT: We shouldn't have taken it from you.

**He offers the sword.**

KULWANT: You can put it back through your mouth if you like.

**The HOLY MAN reaches out and takes the sword.
Beat.**

HOLY MAN: Thank you.
TITOO: Oi, I thought you weren't allowed to speak.
HOLY MAN: Why?
TITOO: Don't you types have a vow of silence or something? He gives you an ice cream and you forget all about religion. Next thing you'll be asking me for a fag.

HOLY MAN: I took no vow of silence.

TITOO: So how come I never heard you talk? You been coming round this way for years.

HOLY MAN: I always had the sword in my mouth.

STALLHOLDER: Didn't it ever rust, the sword – with all your spit on it I mean?

HOLY MAN: I take it out every night and clean it.

**Long beat.**

HOLY MAN: No one ever talked to me.

TITOO: That's 'cause they thought you couldn't.

KULWANT: Would you like another ice cream?

STALLHOLDER: He'll get fat!

TITOO: You want a cigarette?

**The HOLY MAN nods – TITOO gives him a cigarette and a light.**

TITOO: Strange kind of holy man you are.

HOLY MAN: I smoke sometimes. I think I do enough for God.

KULWANT: Are you going to put the sword back in?

HOLY MAN: I feel strange walking around without it.

KULWANT: Is it some kind of special sword?

**Beat. The HOLY MAN looks at him for a moment, as if sizing him up.**

HOLY MAN: It is to me. It means something very special.

KULWANT: What?

HOLY MAN: It means that I have decided to live my life in one way, for one thing only. Without the sword, I would lose my way. My soul would be lost.

KULWANT: Why don't you do a job instead?

HOLY MAN: This is my job – I was appointed to it by God. He came to me in a dream and told me that this was what I was to do.

STALLHOLDER: I hope you got yourself a better pension scheme than me!

HOLY MAN (*ignoring him*): When people see me, they are perhaps reminded of their souls. They remember their connection to the divine.

KULWANT: Oh.

STALLHOLDER: You know something, I think he's right! I'll give all my money to charity and go to work on a leper colony.

TITOO: Yer arms would drop off. Maybe your dick too.

STALLHOLDER: It would be worth it for my ticket to heaven. Perhaps then in my next life I would be born a rich man.

TITOO: I wouldn't want my dick dropping off, not for anything. I run a mile if I see a leper.

KULWANT (*to the* STALLHOLDER): You're going to have another life?

STALLHOLDER: Of course. That's why I have to watch it, I don't want to come back as a donkey or something. I want to come back as a boy from London!

# meredith oakes

## from *The Neighbour*

Meredith Oakes's plays include *The Neighbour* (RNT Studio
Springboards, 1993), *The Editing Process* (Royal Court, 1994)
and *Mind the Gap* (Hampstead Theatre, 1995). She has
written opera libretti for Channel 4 and the ENO and translated
plays by J.M.W. Lenz and Thomas Bernhard for the Gate
Theatre.

**1990s. A London council estate.**

**Around midday.**

**MICHAEL is sitting in a tree near the road. He has a large sports bag. JAMES walks up.**

JAMES: Mike?

MICHAEL: Hullo James.

JAMES: You're in a tree. What's the point of it Michael?

MICHAEL: Waiting for the milk float. Late, ain't it. It's a disgrace.

JAMES: Why aren't you waiting for it in your home?

MICHAEL: I couldn't rob it if I was in my home.

JAMES: Why has that tree got no leaves? You ain't hidden. You're visible. Ain't you got nothing better to do?

MICHAEL: No I fucking ain't.

JAMES: Go down the pub.

MICHAEL: Pub's a fucking shithole.

JAMES: Go down the shop.

MICHAEL: Shop's a fucking rip-off.

JAMES: Go and see your mum.

MICHAEL: Mum's a fucking slag.

JAMES: Go and see your sister.

MICHAEL: She's fucking with my dad.

JAMES: Planning to raid the milk float, are you? Ambush it, will you?

MICHAEL: I'm working it out.

JAMES: Rich pickings there.

MICHAEL: I only need the yoghurts.

JAMES: You want that fucking bifidus, don't you. It's good for your fucking functions.

**MICHAEL is climbing down. He opens his sports bag and takes out a bedding plant which has been uprooted.**

JAMES: That's a pretty flower.

MICHAEL: How many of these have I got?

JAMES: I couldn't really say Michael.

MICHAEL: Forty-two.

JAMES: That's a lot, ain't it.

MICHAEL: When I get them yoghurt pots, I can plant them in and knock them out next Sunday down the market. Two fifty a piece.

JAMES: Where did you get them?

MICHAEL: I been for a walk in the park. The security down there is a joke.

JAMES: The point is, they don't envisage somebody like you.

**SHEILA enters.**

SHEILA: It's no use giving him flowers, Michael, he'll never appreciate you the way I do. You're looking well today, the pair of you. I do like this warm weather, it's so much more modern.

JAMES: It gives me a headache. You got anything for a headache?

SHEILA: I ain't a fucking witch.

JAMES: Go on, you got everything in that bag.

SHEILA: How would you know what I got in my bag? (*She starts to search.*)

JAMES: Could you get the attention of a milkman?

SHEILA: I can't even get the attention of my husband. Here you are. Open wide. (*She feeds him a pill.*)

JAMES: Got any more?

SHEILA: You're like a bleeding baby bird. (*She feeds him another.*)

JAMES: Could you chat him up?

SHEILA: What for?

JAMES: Michael's short of a pint, ain't you Michael.

SHEILA: Why don't I buy him one?

JAMES: No. Tacky.

MICHAEL: Wait up. Here he is.

JAMES (*to* SHEILA): Keep him talking across the road.

SHEILA: I need the loo.

JAMES: Wriggle them hips.

**SHEILA goes. They watch.**

JAMES: What you going to put them in?

**MICHAEL empties the plants out of his sports bag and goes off stage to rob the milk float. Returns a moment later with the bag full of yoghurts.**

JAMES: You're an artist, man. You are so nonchalant. You walked up to that milk like a worker to his machine. You packed that up like you was being paid for it.

MICHAEL: It's fresh here.

JAMES: It's the suspense that made me fart, Michael. Reading the labels, a master stroke.

MICHAEL: I only like the pineapple. I ain't making much on this, all right?

JAMES: Three-way split. Definite.
MICHAEL: Up your arse.

**SHEILA returns.**

SHEILA: Oh James I felt such a fool. 'Where's Canford Street?' I says. 'You're in it,' he says. End of conversation. 'Oh,' says I, 'fancy that, what a stroke of luck.' Then lo and behold he says to me, 'I feel lucky too.' He wants to meet me. He says I got good bones. Don't tell Reg. I wouldn't have good bones after that.

JAMES: I'm good for you, see. I take you out of yourself. I enable you to make new friends.

**Meanwhile MICHAEL has taken off his shirt, and is putting the plants into it and tying it up.**

SHEILA: Did you manage, Michael? Good lord, what's he doing?
JAMES (*takes one of the flowers, breaks off the root, gives her the top*): He's collecting samples. Come on.

**They all leave.**

# judith johnson

## from *Somewhere*

Judith Johnson comes from Liverpool and has been writing plays since 1987. Her work includes *Working Away* (Soho Poly), *Death Party* (Liverpool Everyman), *The Scrappie* (Red Ladder), *Los Escombros* (RNT Education Department), *Somewhere* (Liverpool Playhouse/Royal National Theatre), *Connected* (Wolsey Theatre, Ipswich), *Stone Moon* (BT National Connections) and *Uganda* (Royal Court Theatre Upstairs).

critical mass

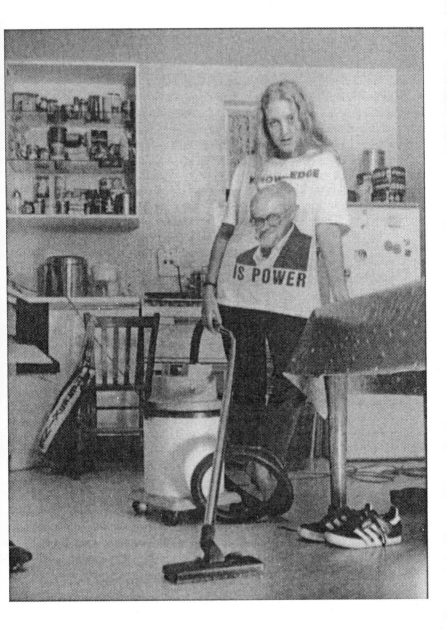

**1981. A small town in the north-west of England.**

**The park.**

**A couple of swings. A grassy bank. CAMPBELL, KEV, SHAUN and LINDA. LINDA
and SHAUN are arm in arm, very lovey-dovey. KEV and CAMPBELL look bored.**

KEV: I'm sick to death of this town. There's fuck all to do. No work, no
money and no decent women.

CAMPBELL: The trouble is all the girls round here are thick as pigshit.

LINDA: Well none of them fancy you Campbell so I shouldn't worry.

SHAUN: Don't worry mate you'll be at college soon, doing your 'A'
Levels, mixing with all the other clever bastards. You can get yourself a
nice girl and you can both talk about books together.

KEV: I wouldn't mind going to college.

LINDA: Only 'cos you've run out of girls to go out with.

KEV: No no. I wouldn't mind doing something. You know. Mechanics or
something.

LINDA: You what? You didn't even manage to turn up for your CSE
Physics exam. Too busy polishing your scooter.

SHAUN: You could go on the YOP scheme. They have mechanics jobs.

KEV: Frig off! I'm no fucking slave.

LINDA: Where is your scooter Kev?

KEV: It's dead.

LINDA: On no, what happened to it? Polish it away to nothing did you?

KEV: No. It's just knackered and I can't fix it.

LINDA: Shame really. All nice and shiny on the outside and falling to bits
on the inside.

KEV: What?

**Pause. KEV kicks the wall rhythmically. CAMPBELL sighs. Enter BARRY and
JONNO.**

JONNO: Evening all!

KEV: Oh. Here come the workers! How was your first day then lads?

JONNO: It was ace. There's some dead fit women working there.

BARRY: Jonno's in love.

JONNO: Ah honest to God Kev you wanna see her. A lifeguard she is. She
looks just like Raquel Welsh. She smiled at me didn't she Barry?

BARRY: I think she might have been laughing actually.

JONNO: No. It was definitely a smile. Looked me straight in the eye she did.

BARRY: She's twenty-one Jonno. You don't stand a chance.

JONNO: She likes me I'm telling you.

KEV: Any more jobs going at the pool?

JONNO: No. They only had work for a couple of people. It's just for the summer like. Keeping it clean while it's busy. We're saving up aren't we Barry?

BARRY: Yeah.

JONNO: We're gonna go to France after we've finished this job. Fruit picking.

KEV: Is it easy to get work in France then?

BARRY: So we're told. There's this lad working at the pool for the summer, a student he is. He said he took a year off like and went travelling. Fruit picking in France, bar work in Greece, he even went to Australia. Slept on the beaches he said. Under the stars. You could do it if you wanted. You could come with us.

KEV: I haven't got any money.

LINDA: You could sell your scooter.

KEV: No I couldn't.

SHAUN: Why not?

KEV: I just couldn't.

LINDA: 'Cos he's a lazy bastard that's why. Can you see him picking grapes all day?

**Enter DAWN and CLARE.**

DAWN: Anyone got any fags?

KEV: Dawn never says hello does she?

CAMPBELL: No. She just starts scrounging.

**DAWN ignores him. BARRY passes DAWN a cigarette. CLARE is very quiet. She goes and sits on a swing.**

BARRY: Here y'are. D'you want one Clare?

CLARE: No ta.

BARRY: Have you give up?

CLARE: No. I just don't feel like one.

BARRY: Oh. OK.

JONNO: Me and Barry started working today Dawn.

DAWN: Oh yeah?

JONNO: We're gonna save up all our money and go fruit picking in September, aren't we Barry?

BARRY: That's the plan.

DAWN: Are you leaving us Barry?

BARRY: 'Fraid so babes.

DAWN: Oh no! What will I do without you?

BARRY (*serious*): You can come with us if you like.

DAWN: Well you know I would, but me and Clare have got our own plans, haven't we Clare?

CLARE: Yeah.

BARRY: Oh yeah? What's that?

DAWN: We're going to Manchester aren't we? To live with our Jane.

BARRY: Manchester?

DAWN: Yeah. We're gonna make a load of money.

BARRY: Doing what?

DAWN: Escort work. My cousin Jane, she works for an escort agency.

JONNO: What's one of them?

LINDA: Oh you just have to look after businessmen for an evening, don't you Dawn?

SHAUN: What d'you mean look after them?

DAWN: You go for a meal with them or to a club or something. Talk to them you know. Keep them company.

JONNO: How d'you mean keep them company?

LINDA: You don't have to have sex with them or anything Jonno. But sometimes they ask though, don't they Dawn?

SHAUN: You seem to know an awful lot about this.

LINDA: That's 'cos we done it last time we went to see Jane.

SHAUN: You done what?!

LINDA: Don't worry. We just went out for a meal with some blokes. Nothing else.

SHAUN: Hang on. Let me get this right. You went out with two businessmen for a meal and they paid you just for being there?

LINDA: That's right.

SHAUN: Christ!

DAWN: It's just a bit of female company for them.

KEV: Can't they get women without paying for them?

DAWN: Not as nice as us.

KEV: Not as young as you, you mean.

LINDA: We didn't go to bed with them you know.

BARRY (*changing the subject sharpish*): Well. It looks like we're all off somewhere anyway.

LINDA: I'm not.

SHAUN: Neither am I.

LINDA: That's alright then!

**They embrace.**

JONNO: Christ. Will you put her down Shaun? You never stop you two.

CAMPBELL: How you feeling anyway Dawn?

DAWN: Eh?

CAMPBELL: I hear you and Lee Kelly had a drinking contest.

KEV: Oh yeah? Who won?

CAMPBELL: Lee Kelly was sick, but not Dawn. Takes after her mum, don't you?

DAWN: You what?

CAMPBELL: You heard.

DAWN: Don't talk about my mother Campbell.

CAMPBELL: You both like your drink don't you?

DAWN: I said don't fuckin' talk about my mother.

CAMPBELL: Oh dear. Touched a sore spot have I?

**DAWN goes for him. She grabs him by his collar and pulls him down so he falls on the floor. She goes to kick him in the balls but BARRY pulls her away. Enter LEE KELLY.**

CAMPBELL: You fuckin' bitch.

DAWN: You're the bitch Campbell.

KEV (*to* CAMPBELL): Come on. Let's go.

**He pulls CAMPBELL to his feet and they exit.**

DAWN (*shouting after him*): Bastard!

BARRY: Calm down Dawn.

LEE: What's up with him?

DAWN: He hates me, that's what.

LINDA: I reckon he fancies you. That's why he's always getting at you.

DAWN: Oh I don't think it's me he fancies.

SHAUN: He was getting at Linda before, wasn't he Lind?

LINDA: Yeah. He was a bit like.

DAWN: It's 'cos we've both been out with Kev.

SHAUN: You what?

DAWN: It's Kev. He loves Kev.

JONNO: What d'you mean?

DAWN: I mean he loves Kev.

LEE: Did he hit you Dawn?

DAWN: He was saying things about me mum.

LEE: I'll have a word with him.

DAWN: No. You're alright. I think he got the message.

**DAWN and LEE focus all their conversation on each other forgetting the others who listen in. BARRY moves away from DAWN.**

LEE: You should take no notice of him.

DAWN: Yeah. S'pose so. He just winds me up that's all. How are you anyway? Still feeling sick?

LEE (*smiling*): Feeling a lot better ta. How about you?

DAWN: Oh. I'm fine.

**She returns his smile. LINDA and JONNO exchange a knowing look.**

CLARE: Dawn. I'm gonna go home, I don't feel very well.

DAWN: Oh.

**She glances at LEE.**

DAWN: Alright babes. I'll come with you.

CLARE: No. You're alright, you stay here.

DAWN: No. I'll walk you home.

CLARE: You don't have to.

DAWN: I want to.

LEE: Er. D'you mind if I come too?

DAWN: No. Come if you like.

**DAWN and CLARE start to exit.**

DAWN: Come head then.

**LEE follows them. The others start to exit in the opposite direction.**

LINDA: Christ. Did you hear that? (*Putting on a posh voice.*) 'D'you mind if I come too?' I've never heard Lee Kelly talk like that before.

JONNO: He's different isn't he? From when he was at school. He's quieter. Doesn't take the piss so much.

SHAUN: I still wouldn't mess with him tho'.

JONNO: No. Neither would I.

BARRY: He just fancies Dawn that's all.

JONNO: What difference does that make? We all fancy Dawn, Barry.

BARRY: The difference Jonno, is that she fancies him back.

JONNO: Well she fancied Kev back didn't she. He didn't start saying nice things to her and all that.

BARRY: Well maybe he should have, he might have got more than a quick thrill out of her.

JONNO: Eh? What d'you mean?

BARRY: Oh nothing.

JONNO: You always have to stick up for her don't you?

BARRY: She sticks up for herself Jonno.

**They exit. Enter KEV and CAMPBELL. They're halfway through a bottle of woodpecker cider. CAMPBELL sits on a swing. KEV hands him the bottle and he finishes it off.**

KEV (*watching* CAMPBELL): Better?

CAMPBELL: Yeah. Stupid cow.

KEV: You shouldn't have gone on about her mam y'know.

CAMPBELL: Why not? Everybody knows about it.

KEV: Yeah but . . .

CAMPBELL: Yeah but what? She thinks she's the fuckin' Queen of Sheba.

KEV: She's just a girl Campbell. Don't get yourself so worked up.

CAMPBELL: You're just the same as the rest of them. Creepin' round her like she's Debbie fuckin' Harry.

KEV: No I'm not.

CAMPBELL: You shoulda seen your face when she necked you on Friday night. Like a little dog, and she'd just threw you a bone.

KEV (*grinning*): Bone's the right word mate. She can't half kiss.

CAMPBELL: That wasn't for you. That was for Lee Kelly's benefit. She fancies Lee, Kev. She's not interested in you.

KEV: She was interested enough after the Specials concert. She made me take her to the park. She asked me Campbell.

CAMPBELL: Yeah but your Scooter was working then wasn't it? I'll give her six months and she'll be picking up kerb crawlers in Manchester just like her Jane.

KEV: What you going on about?

CAMPBELL: Nothing.

KEV: Nothing!

CAMPBELL: I'm not meant to say.

KEV: Come head Campbell. You can't just say something like that then shut your mouth.

CAMPBELL: It's something me dad told me.

KEV: Come on!

CAMPBELL: Well. He helped Dawn's cousin Jane. She come to see him at the Advice Bureau. She got picked up for soliciting and she reckons the bizzies knocked her about a bit.

KEV: Jesus! So that's what Dawn gets up to when she goes to Manchester.

CAMPBELL: You mustn't tell anyone Kev.

KEV: Jesus. Shit!

CAMPBELL: What?

KEV: I might have caught something off her.

CAMPBELL: Eh?

KEV: After the Madness concert.

CAMPBELL: Don't be stupid. Anyway she's just as likely to catch something off you.

KEV: You what?

CAMPBELL: You heard.

KEV: What you trying to say? I'm not a fuckin' whore.

CAMPBELL: Well you're not exactly Mr Monogamous are you?

KEV: What's that supposed to mean?

CAMPBELL: Well, you know. You sleep around just as much as she does.

KEV: Don't fuckin' use your big college words on me mate.

CAMPBELL: I didn't mean . . .

KEV: Girls like me. They just like me OK?

CAMPBELL: OK.

KEV: They fancy me.

CAMPBELL: Yes. OK. I only meant . . .

KEV: You're gonna have to stop getting so jealous you know.

**A slight pause.**

CAMPBELL: Jealous of what?

KEV: You'll get yourself a girlfriend one day.

CAMPBELL: Oh. I see.

KEV: Yeah. They're not your type round here that's all. There's nothing wrong with you or anything.

CAMPBELL: I'm not jealous Kev.

KEV: Wait till you get to college mate, they'll be all over you then.

CAMPBELL: Kev. I'm not jealous of you. You're me mate OK? Me best mate. I'm not fuckin' jealous!

KEV: Alright. Keep your hair on!

**Pause. Embarrassment.**

CAMPBELL: Kev?

KEV: What?

**Pause.**

KEV: What?

CAMPBELL: Don't you ever . . .

**Pause.**

CAMPBELL: Don't you ever . . .

**Pause.**

KEV: Don't I ever what?

CAMPBELL: Oh nothing. It doesn't matter.

**Pause. They're both a bit embarrassed.**

KEV: So. Did she win the case then?

CAMPBELL: Eh?

KEV: Dawn's cousin.

CAMPBELL: Oh. No. Not a chance. Her word against the bizzies weren't it? Me dad told her not to bother.

KEV: Fuckin' tart.

CAMPBELL: She was covered from head to toe in bruises.

KEV: What does she expect? Women like that. They deserve it.

**Pause.**

KEV: You got any weed?

CAMPBELL: In the house.

KEV: Well, what we doing here then? Let's go and have a smoke.

CAMPBELL: Yeah. Alright then Kev. Let's go and have a smoke.

**They exit. Enter DAWN, followed by LEE. DAWN sits down. LEE sits beside her.**

DAWN: Did you used to come here when you were little Lee? Me and Clare did. There was a roundabout wasn't there? Remember when they built the wooden castle?

LEE: Yeah. We burnt it down.

DAWN: We didn't go in the playground much. We used to come to this bit 'cos we liked the trees. We'd lie down and look at the sky through the leaves and then we'd levitate.

LEE: You what?

DAWN: We used to rise out of our bodies and float up to the sky.

LEE: Fuck off!

DAWN: No honest. It works. You just have to think really hard in your head. And you have to really want to do it. Come on.

**She lies down.**

LEE: Er. What you doing?

DAWN: Levitating. Come on Lee.

**LEE lies down beside her. He looks a bit unsure.**

DAWN: Just look up at the stars and think about floating up through the trees.

LEE: I done this once when I was really stoned.

DAWN: You don't have to be stoned.

LEE: It might help.

DAWN: Shush!

**They lie still and try to levitate.**

LEE (*after a bit*): Dawn?

DAWN: Shush!

**He sits up.**

LEE: I can't concentrate.

DAWN: It was just starting to work. You're not trying hard enough.

**LEE puts his hand out and touches DAWN's face. She pushes his hand away
and sits up.**

DAWN: Don't Lee.

**Pause. LEE turns away from her.**

DAWN: Got any ciggies?
LEE: What's this all about Dawn?
DAWN (*not looking at him*): What d'you mean?
LEE: You know. This weird act. You ask me to come back to the park
with you, I don't expect to be lying down trying to levitate.
DAWN: What **do** you expect?
LEE: I dunno, I . . .
DAWN: A quick fuck, is that what you want? OK then. Come on.

**She grabs hold of him. Starts trying to undo his fly. She is very angry. He
tries to push her away.**

DAWN: Come on. I'll lie down on the grass shall I and open me legs for
you so you can get inside me. Is that what you want to do 'cos I can do that
for you Lee, that's easy.

**He pushes her off.**

LEE: Stop it will you. Jesus. What's up with you?
DAWN (*getting up*): I'm going home.
LEE (*grabs her arm*): Don't.
DAWN: Why not? 'Cos you haven't got your end away yet?
LEE: No! Can't we just sit down and talk?

**Pause. She looks hard at him. He still holds her arm.**

LEE: Come on Dawn.
DAWN: Let go of me arm.

**He does so. She sits down beside him.**

LEE: I just don't know what's going on that's all.
DAWN: I wanted to levitate.
LEE: I thought you were taking the piss.
DAWN: No. No. I wasn't.

**Pause.**

DAWN: It's just . . . I'm worried about Clare.

LEE: She's alright.

DAWN: She's not.

LEE: She's just sad about her grandad dying. She's bound to be.

DAWN: She's so quiet. She gets really depressed sometimes. Even before he died.

LEE: She'll be alright.

DAWN: I don't know what's going on in her head.

LEE: She'll be alright Dawn. Don't worry about it.

**Pause.**

DAWN: You're quiet too.

LEE: I don't know what to say to you.

DAWN: No. I mean compared with how you used to be. Before they chucked you out of school.

LEE: Yeah well. I've been doing a lot of thinking since then.

DAWN: About what?

LEE: About life.

DAWN: Have you come up with anything?

LEE: Yeah.

DAWN: What?

LEE: I've decided to join the Army.

**Pause.**

DAWN: You don't have to do that.

LEE: What else can I do?

DAWN: Working on the bin wagons is better than that.

LEE: There aren't any jobs going on the bin wagons.

**Pause.**

LEE: Me dad's kicked me out. He said he was sick of me hanging around the house doing nothing. Getting in the way. Causing trouble. We had a fight. He tried to hit me mum again and I tried to stop him. It's always the same. He comes back, crawling on his hands and knees, begging for forgiveness. She puts her arms round him like he's a little baby or something. Fucking cunt.

DAWN: Where you living?

LEE: At Barry's till the end of this week. Till his mum and dad come back.

DAWN: What you gonna do after that?

LEE: Dunno. Kip in the park till I join the Army and get away from this fuckin' town.

DAWN: You don't have to be a hard case y'know Lee.

LEE: It's either that or be a nobody Dawn.

**Silence. DAWN moves towards him. She takes his hand and holds it against her face.**

DAWN: You can come and stay with me.

LEE: Your mum'd love that.

DAWN: She won't mind.

LEE: Won't she?

DAWN: She's not sober very often but when she is she understands.

LEE: Understands what?

DAWN: Understands me.

LEE: What's that on your arm?

DAWN: It's a tattoo. Jonno did it for me.

LEE: It says Special.

DAWN: The Specials.

LEE (*smiling*): Oh yeah.

**She takes LEE's hand and moves it slowly down her body till it rests between her legs.**

DAWN (*whispers*): Touch me Lee.

**LEE moves forward to do so. The lights fade out.**

# jonathan harvey
## from *Beautiful Thing*

Jonathan Harvey's first play, *The Cherry Blossom Tree*, was produced at Liverpool Playhouse Studio in 1987, when he was eighteen. He has since written *Mohair* (Royal Court Young Writers' Festival, 1988), *Tripping and Falling* (Glasshouse Theatre Co., Manchester, 1989), *Catch* (Spring Street Studio, Hull, 1990), *Lady Snogs the Blues* (Lincoln Arts Festival, 1991), *Wildfire* (Royal Court Theatre Upstairs, 1992), *Beautiful Thing* (Bush Theatre, 1993, Donmar Warehouse/Duke of York's, 1994), *Babies* (Royal Court, 1994) and *Boom Bang-a-Bang* (Bush Theatre, 1995). He has won the George Devine Award, the John Whiting Award and the *Evening Standard* Most Promising Playwright Award.

**The play is set in Thamesmead, south-east London, in May 1993.**

JAMIE's **bedroom. The early hours of the morning, a few nights later.**
**Complete blackness.** JAMIE **is in bed.** SANDRA **comes in, in the dark.**

SANDRA: Jamie? You awake? Jamie I know you are.

JAMIE: What?

SANDRA: Where've you been please?

JAMIE: Nowhere.

SANDRA: Oh yeah? It's half-one in the morning actually. (*Pause.*) Where did you go?

JAMIE: Out.

SANDRA: Jamie!

**She bends and switches on his bedside light.** JAMIE **doesn't move, lying with his back to her.**

SANDRA: You went the Gloucester din't ya? Look at me.

JAMIE **rolls over.**

JAMIE: Only went for a drink.

SANDRA: That's where gay people go. They go there and they go Macmillan's in Deptford.

JAMIE: It's not just gay people who go. Other people go.

SANDRA: People like you?

JAMIE: Yeah?

SANDRA: It's no time for lying Jamie.

JAMIE: It's not a lie.

SANDRA: I had a phone call tonight.

JAMIE: Oh you're lucky.

SANDRA: From your tutor.

JAMIE: Miss Ellis?

SANDRA: She's worried about ya.

JAMIE: God, coz I bunk off games does it mean I'm gay?

SANDRA: No. Coz someone hit you.

JAMIE: Everyone gets hit.

SANDRA: And called you queer. And it aint the first time. She's worried about what it's doing to ya.

JAMIE: I'm all right.

SANDRA: Are you Jamie? Coz I'm not sure you are. I mean, what am I supposed to think? When you're . . . you're going out drinking and coming home at half-one. Getting hit, getting moody, I don't think you are.

JAMIE: Well I am so go back to bed!

SANDRA: Er, I'll go when I'm good and ready if you don't mind.

JAMIE: I'm tired.

SANDRA: You're pissed.

JAMIE: No I'm not.

SANDRA: Pissed from a bloody gay bar!

JAMIE: How d'you know it's gay anyway?

SANDRA: Coz it's got a bloody great big pink neon arse outside of it. Jamie, I'm in the business, I get to know these things!

JAMIE: You been spying on me?

SANDRA: No. Someone at work seen you go in. . .

JAMIE: Don't mean I'm gay . . .

SANDRA: Going in with another boy, so who was that?

JAMIE (*beat*): Ste.

SANDRA: Ste? Right.

JAMIE: Still don't mean I'm gay. They wanna mind their own business.

SANDRA: That's what I said.

JAMIE: Well then, what you goin' on at me for?

SANDRA: Because sometimes Jamie, I can put two and two together and make bloody four, I'm not stupid you know.

JAMIE: I never said you were!

SANDRA: So I think I deserve an explanation.

JAMIE: I went for a drink. Big deal. Everyone in my class goes drinking.

SANDRA: Yeah but they don't all go the bloody Gloucester though do they!

JAMIE: Some of 'em take drugs, at least I'm not doing that!

SANDRA: I bloody hope you're not!

JAMIE: Ah well thanks a lot. Thanks a bundle. Go back to bed!

SANDRA: I can't sleep Jamie!

JAMIE: Well don't take it out on me.

SANDRA: Jamie. Will you just talk to me?!

JAMIE: I'm knackered.

SANDRA: Please Jamie. Talk to me.

JAMIE: What about?

SANDRA (*sitting on bed*): I'm your mother.

**Pause.**

JAMIE: Some things are hard to say.

SANDRA: I know. I know that, Jamie . . .

JAMIE (*crying now*): I'm not weird if that's what you're thinking!

SANDRA: I know you're not love.

JAMIE: You think I'm too young. You think it's just a phase. You think I'm . . . I'm gonna catch AIDS and . . . and everything!

SANDRA: You know a lot about me don't ya? Jesus you wanna get on that Mastermind. Specialised subject – Your Mother. Don't cry. I'm not gonna put you out like an empty bottle in the morning. Jesus, I thought you knew me well enough to know that. Why couldn't you talk to me eh? Going behind my back like that, getting up to allsorts. There's me going to bed of a night feeling sorry for ya, coz you had to share a bed with Ste. And . . . and all the time you were . . . you were doing a seventy minus one . . .

JAMIE: What?

SANDRA: Think about it.

JAMIE **tuts.**

SANDRA: Do you talk to him?

JAMIE: Me and him's the same.

SANDRA: He's sixteen years of age Jamie. What pearls of wisdom can he throw your way? He aint seen life. He's never even had a holiday.

JAMIE: It's difficult init.

SANDRA: Am I that much of a monster?

JAMIE: No!

SANDRA: Don't get me wrong. I like the lad. Always have. All I'm saying is he's young.

JAMIE: He's good to me.

SANDRA: Is he?

JAMIE: Yeah.

SANDRA **is bottling up the tears. She can't bring herself to cry in front of** JAMIE. **She gets up quickly and runs out of the room. She comes onto the walkway and starts to cry.** JAMIE **bawls.** TONY **comes into** JAMIE's **room.**

TONY: What's up?

JAMIE: Go away.

TONY: What have you done now?

JAMIE: Nothing!

TONY: Then why's she so upset?

JAMIE: I'm a queer! A bender! A pufter! A knobshiner! Brownhatter! Shirtflaplifter!

TONY: I get the picture.

JAMIE: Leave me alone.

TONY: And she knows this.

JAMIE: No, I thought I'd tell you first.

TONY: This is . . . it's . . . it's okay. Night kidder.

JAMIE: Yeah.

**TONY leaves the room and comes out onto the walkway where SANDRA stands crying. It is dark on the walkway, except for a thin shaft of light which creeps across from SANDRA's open door.**

TONY: There's no need to cry.

SANDRA: Oh isn't there?!

TONY: It's okay, I know. It's natural. (*Pause.*) You like tomatoes. I like beetroot.

SANDRA: Shut up.

TONY: Hey I'm not saying it's easy, yeah? No way. (*Tries to cuddle her.*)

SANDRA (*wriggling free*): Off of me.

TONY: I know. That's cool.

**SANDRA gets some fags out of her pocket and a lighter. She lights up, her hands shaking. She wipes her face as she speaks.**

SANDRA: He was . . . he was the most beautiful baby in Bermondsey you know. Pushed him round. In his little frilly hat. In a big blue pram called Queen o' the Road. Oh fuckin'ell.

TONY: None of that's changed.

SANDRA: State o'me.

TONY: Just let it out Sandra.

SANDRA: Shut up.

TONY: You're fighting it hon.

SANDRA: Fighting? I've been fighting all me life. Kids pickin' on 'im – I was there. Council saying bollocks to benefit, I was there. When I had three pee in me purse and an empty fridge I went robbin' for that boy.

And you say I'm fighting. You! What have you ever had to fight for in your life?!

TONY: Come here.

SANDRA: I'm all right.

TONY: Sandra . . .

SANDRA: Go back to bed Tony.

TONY: You need support.

SANDRA: I wanna be on me own.

TONY: No.

SANDRA: Yes.

TONY: If you're sure.

SANDRA: I'm sure.

TONY: Well . . . I'll be waiting.

**TONY submits. He's ready to go back in when LEAH's door swings open and LEAH steps out, her door swinging shut behind her. She holds an egg whisk to her chest. She steps forward. When she speaks she does so in a deep South American drawl. She is tripping on acid. TONY is waylaid by her.**

LEAH (*to* TONY): Not so fast! This is my big speech.

SANDRA: Oh for crying out loud.

TONY: Huh?

LEAH: I've never won anything in my life before. Certainly not Slimmer of the Year.

**LEAH clears her throat. SANDRA and TONY look to each other, then to LEAH.**

LEAH: Thank you to all members of the Academy. This means so much. I'd like to thank my manager, the wonderful Ted Bow-Locks. And my band, they're all here . . . (*Waves to* TONY.) Hi guys! I'd like to thank Jesus Christ for coming to earth. I'd like to thank the President for being great . . . but most of all I'd like to thank one very special person . . .

SANDRA: What the . . .

LEAH: The woman from whom all energy flows. This award is as much hers as mine. The woman who gives me so much . . . inspiration. Let's hear it for . . . Mama San!

SANDRA: Leah?

LEAH: People say to me, they say . . .

SANDRA: Leah are you drunk?

LEAH: Where do you get your energy from?

SANDRA: Leah it's half-one in the morning.

TONY: Has she taken something?

LEAH: And I say 'Hey! Mama San!'

SANDRA (*to* LEAH): Is your mother in?

LEAH: Mama San! Git down honey! Your vibes are shootin' right through of me!

SANDRA: Is she working nights?

LEAH: Don't let the light leave you Mama San.

SANDRA (*goes to* LEAH's *door and bangs on it*): Rose? (*To* LEAH.) Get your keys out. Hurry up.

TONY (*to* LEAH): Have you taken, like, a trip, you know?

SANDRA (*tuts. Calls through to her flat*): Jamie?! Leah, have you got your key please?!

TONY: Don't shout at her!

LEAH: You're giving me bad vibes Mama!

TONY: She's on something.

SANDRA: Jamie!!

LEAH (*to* TONY): You're an old, old man. And I don't like old men.

TONY: That's cool. That's no problem.

SANDRA: It is a problem actually Tony. Don't pander to her.

TONY: I'm not pandering to her.

LEAH: Panda? Where's the panda.

**JAMIE comes to the door.**

JAMIE: What now?

LEAH (*spies an imaginary panda*): Oh there he is! Hello!

SANDRA: Jamie does she take anything?

JAMIE: What like?

TONY: Look we're not talking aspirin, here, right?

JAMIE: Drugs?

SANDRA: Jesus.

JAMIE: Dunno.

SANDRA: Get her key off her Tony.

**LEAH is caught up in looking closely at SANDRA's hanging basket.**

TONY: We mustn't touch her.

SANDRA:  Get her away from my special basket Tony! You're being too easy on her!

TONY:  No, we'll freak her out!

SANDRA:  She's freaking me out Tony!

JAMIE:  What you taken Leah?

SANDRA:  I've never seen anything so ridiculous in all me life. (*Grabs* LEAH.) Leah! Give us your bloody key!

**LEAH whimpers and fights for breath. TONY grabs SANDRA's arm.**

TONY:  Sandra!

SANDRA:  Er, body language Tony! (*Struggles with him.*)

JAMIE:  Look at her!

LEAH (*slipping to floor*): I'm dead. Dead and buried. (*Flops to floor.*)

TONY:  Look what you've done now.

SANDRA:  I don't believe you just did that Tony.

JAMIE:  What's she doing?

SANDRA:  I'll have a nice bruise in the morning thanks to you.

TONY:  Christ, er, I saw a video about Woodstock once. What do we do?

SANDRA:  I've got a nice suggestion, but there's children present.

TONY:  We can't leave her there all night!

SANDRA/JAMIE:  Why not?!

**STE comes out of his flat in his bed gear, the light from his flat brightening the walkway.**

STE:  What's the noise?

SANDRA:  Oh let's make a party of it shall we?

JAMIE:  You don't know anything that's good for drug addicts do ya?

STE:  What?

TONY:  She's not a drug addict!

SANDRA:  And my name's Wincey Willis! (*To* STE.) Tony thinks she's taken acid. And Tony knows these sorts o'things coz he's that way inclined hisself I wouldn't wonder.

STE:  Orange juice. (*Everyone looks to* STE.) Me brother says if you have a bad trip on acid, drink orange juice.

JAMIE:  'Ere, it might be that Ecstasy! Everyone takes that round here.

TONY:  It's not Ecstasy.

SANDRA:  Oh really?

TONY:  No, the symptoms are all wrong.

JAMIE: Have you got any orange?

SANDRA: No.

STE: We have.

TONY: Will you get it?

STE: Yeah.

**Exits.**

SANDRA (*to* TONY): Proper little Doctor Dolittle intya?

TONY: I don't need this right now Sandra.

SANDRA: Oh and I do? I'm telling ya, I'll be glad to get outa this bloody place.

TONY: Can we just keep the noise down?

JAMIE: What d'you mean Mum?

SANDRA: Oh and I suppose you like standing out on the landing at two in the morning? Surrounded by drug experts and the like.

TONY: Oh loosen up Sandra.

SANDRA: Oh you can shut up Tony if you don't mind.

TONY (*to* JAMIE): Your mother's tired.

SANDRA: I said shut up, didn't I?

**STE comes back with a carton of fresh orange. He hands it to TONY. TONY leans over LEAH. The others watch, fascinated.**

TONY: Leah? (*Pause.*) Leah? (*Still no response.*) Mama Cass?

LEAH (*immediately lifts her head. Conspiratorially*): I know they're all talking about me. I know it. But what do you expect? This is the price of fame. Ask any of the greats, they'll tell you: Betty, Joan, Marilyn.

TONY (*holding carton out*): I've got a beautiful drink here. And if you drink it, you'll have the time of your life.

LEAH: Really?

TONY: It's the best.

LEAH: You see the problem is . . . you have seventeen heads. And my mother made me swear that I'd never take a drink off a guy with seventeen heads.

SANDRA (*to* JAMIE): I'm sorry, this is knocking me sick now.

TONY: Right. Ste, you try.

STE: No.

JAMIE: Go on Ste, give it a try.

STE (*steps forward. To* JAMIE): Wish me luck.

JAMIE: Ata boy Ste.

**SANDRA watches this exchange with interest. TONY hands STE the drink. SANDRA stares at JAMIE, then round to LEAH.**

LEAH: Mm. Pretty boy.

STE (*to* LEAH): Right . . . see this right . . . you know if you drink it, you'll feel better. D'you know what I mean?

LEAH (*giggles to* TONY): Is he a fan or something?

TONY: Yes.

LEAH: Mmh!

TONY (*to* STE): Call her Mama Cass!

JAMIE (*laughs*): Gutted!

STE: No.

TONY (*grabs carton*): Mama Cass?

LEAH (*takes carton and drinks some*): Why sir! Your juice tastes mighty fine to me!

TONY: Have some more.

**They all watch as LEAH drinks. As she does, SANDRA speaks.**

SANDRA: There's a pub up in Rotherhithe. The Anchor. The brewery want me to be temporary licensee. (*They all, bar* LEAH, *look to* SANDRA.) It's got a little beer garden, and a piano. And you can watch the boats go up and down on the Thames. And it's got a nice little flat above it. Room for a family.

LEAH (*to* TONY): Are you in the band?

TONY: No.

LEAH: Yes you are.

TONY: Yes. I am.

JAMIE: Why didn't you tell me?

LEAH: You know, you're very good.

SANDRA: You were out.

TONY: Cheers.

LEAH: You're a very beautiful person.

JAMIE: But . . .

LEAH: Am I a beautiful person?

TONY: Yes. You're immensely beautiful.

JAMIE: You coulda told me before.

SANDRA: Snap! Tony, how long's this gonna take?

STE: Ten hours.

SANDRA: What?!

JAMIE: Blimey!

SANDRA: Ten hours?

STE: I think so. I dunno. That's what I've been told. I don't do it. Respect meself too much.

SANDRA: Her mother won't be back till breakfast.

TONY: We'll have to take her inside.

SANDRA: Oh brilliant.

JAMIE: She's not getting in with me!

SANDRA: I hope you don't think I'm sitting up with her Tony, coz I'm telling you now . . .

TONY: I'll sit up with her. It'll be all right. I'm good with kids.

LEAH: What's happening?

TONY: Why don't you come into this nice house with me?

LEAH: Mama . . .

TONY: Mama . . .

LEAH: Mm. I don't know.

TONY: You'll love the wallpaper.

SANDRA: Oh thanks.

TONY: Here.

**Holds out his hand so she can take it. The others stand aside so TONY can lead LEAH in. She looks at them.**

LEAH: Please . . . no autographs.

**TONY and LEAH step inside.**

TONY (*off*): Isn't it nice?

LEAH (*off*): Groovy patterns, wow!

SANDRA: Right, the show's over. We can all get in now.

JAMIE: You played a blinder there Ste.

SANDRA: Jamie. I want you in.

JAMIE: I'm just talking to Ste.

SANDRA: You got school in the morning.

JAMIE: No I haven't. Tomorrow's Saturday.

STE: Time for my beauty sleep anyway.

JAMIE: Ste, she knows.

SANDRA: Who's she? The cat's mother?

JAMIE: Me mum knows.

**Pause. STE looks horrified. His lower lip starts to tremble.**

STE: You gonna tell my dad? (*Cries.*)

SANDRA: No.

STE: Oh my God . . .

SANDRA: Oh don't you start, I said no, didn't I?

JAMIE: Ste it's all right. (*Attempts to put his arm around* STE, *who shrugs him off.*)

STE: Jamie . . .

SANDRA: Jamie . . .

JAMIE: Ste . . .

SANDRA: Steven, stop crying please. I am not going to tell your dad.

STE (*to* JAMIE): Why d'you have to go and grass?

SANDRA: Please Steven.

JAMIE: I never!

STE: Yeah well how come she knows?

SANDRA: Coz SHE never come down with the last shower! Jamie get 'im an 'anky. There's a box of autumnal shades by my bed.

**JAMIE goes inside.**

SANDRA: Jesus Ste will you stop crying? I don't believe in secrets. I like people to be straight up and honest. But I'm no fool. D'you think I want these flats to be infamous for child murder? No. So I won't be telling your dad.

STE: He'd kill me!

SANDRA: Yes. I've just said that.

STE: No he would.

SANDRA: I think we've established that already actually Ste.

STE: They all would, all of 'em.

SANDRA: I'LL bloody kill you in a minute if you don't stop snivelling and shut up! You're a good lad. That's what counts. And . . . somewhere you'll find people what won't kill you.

STE: No I won't.

SANDRA: Well you've found the Gloucester.

STE: I hate it.

SANDRA: Yeah well somewhere else then, shut up.

STE: There aint nowhere else.

SANDRA: There is actually Steven, coz there's an island in the Mediterranean called 'Lesbian', and all its inhabitants are dykes. So I think you got your eye wiped there.

**JAMIE comes out with a box of hankies**.

SANDRA: Now. Wipe 'em properly.

JAMIE: There.

STE: Tar. I'm sorry.

JAMIE: Don't be a dickhead.

STE: Fuck me.

SANDRA: Er, there'll be none o'that out here thank you. (*To* JAMIE.) Are you gonna be long out here?

JAMIE: No.

STE: No Sandra.

SANDRA: Well . . .

STE: We won't Sandra. I'm going to bed. Honest Sandra.

SANDRA: That's me name Ste, don't wear it out. Night Steven. (*Goes in.*)

STE: Night.

**SANDRA exits.**

JAMIE: What's Leah like eh?

STE: I know.

JAMIE: Jees!

STE: She's blinding your mum.

JAMIE: She's all right.

STE: Init? Who else knows?

JAMIE: Only Tony. (*Pause.*) Give us a kiss.

STE: No!

JAMIE: Let's go the stairs, no one can see there.

STE: There's no such thing as just a kiss. I'll knock you up in the morning, yeah?

JAMIE (*Christine Cagney*): Knock away Marybeth, knock away!

STE: See you Christine.

**STE goes to his door. JAMIE stays where he is and watches. STE turns round.**

STE: What?

JAMIE: Watching.

STE:  What?!

JAMIE:  You!

STE  (*points to* JAMIE's *door and orders him to move*): Now!

**Reluctantly JAMIE goes. Both doors close.**

# patrick marber

## from *Dealer's Choice*

Patrick Marber was born in London in 1964. He has worked as a writer and performer in the radio and TV programmes *On The Hour, The Day Today, Knowing Me, Knowing You, Paul Calf Video Diary* and *Pauline Calf Video Diary*. *Dealer's Choice* is his first stage play and opened in his own production at the Royal National Theatre in February 1995 before transferring to the Vaudeville Theatre.

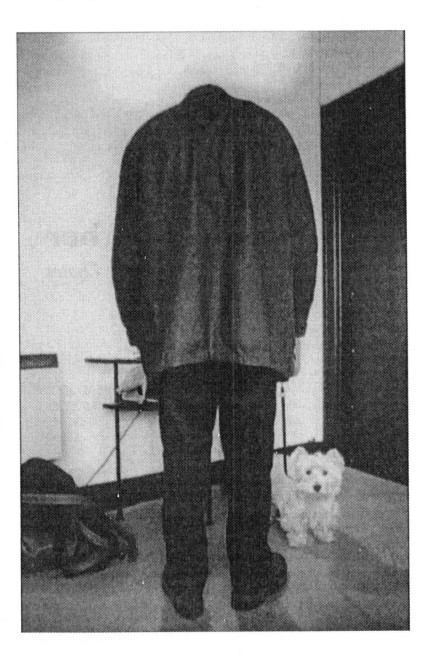

**Split set. Kitchen. Restaurant.**
**It is midnight. The restaurant is closed. The staff are all itching to start**
**their regular Sunday night poker game but one of the customers, ASH, is**
**still sitting at his table.**

**Restaurant.**

CARL: So how's it going?
ASH: Yeah OK.
CARL: Did you meet my father?
ASH: Yeah.
CARL: As I said? Anal or what?
ASH: He's OK.
CARL: Yeah he's OK.
ASH: I had a nice meal.
CARL: Great.
ASH: You got the money?
CARL: Not all of it.
ASH: How much have you got?
CARL: Two hundred and sixty-five.

**Pause.**

ASH: You owe me four grand.

**Beat.**

ASH: Where is it?
CARL: It's . . . gone.
ASH: What do you mean it's gone?
CARL: Casino, I've just been. I lost it. I had two grand, I tried to win the
other two playing blackjack, the dealer was on a freak roll. I was playing
hundred quid a box . . . I was trying to count like you taught me . . . he
was hitting aces and tens non-stop.

**Beat.**

CARL: Are you going to kill me?
ASH: Jesus, he thinks he's in a movie.

**Beat.**

ASH: I told you it had to be tonight.

CARL: I know.

ASH: I've been telling you for three months you had to pay it tonight.

CARL: I know.

ASH: I owe this money.

CARL: I know.

ASH: I have to go to a game now and pay this money.

CARL: I know.

ASH: Alright fine, you said you could get it off your father, go and get it off your father.

CARL: I'm sorry, I can't.

ASH: Listen fuckbrain, you go to your nice father now and you tell him what a sad sorry little prick you are for spunking all this money and you tell him the truth and promise him you'll never gamble again because you're a fucking loser and you get me my money. Now.

CARL: I can't.

ASH: You have to.

CARL: I can't get the money.

ASH: You have to get the money.

CARL: And what if I can't?

ASH: They'll come in here with big guns and blow your brains out. You fucking idiot. It's serious. It's a poker debt. It has to be paid. You said, you said when I lent you this, this year, all this year, you said your father was a soft touch, your father the rich businessman with his swank restaurant. You said he'd give you the money if it came to it. This is it. Go get the money, go crying, go begging, go suck his fucking cock I don't care, just get the fucking money.

**Beat.**

ASH: You want me to go in there and get it?

CARL: No, he doesn't know about the gambling. I can't . . . it would kill him. Ash I do love him, he's my father.

ASH: You think I care?

CARL: Yes. Come on . . . you like me.

ASH: Like is irrelevant.

CARL: Please . . .

ASH: Can't do it Carl. This is fucked up. Get the money.

CARL: Please don't make me.

ASH:  Right I'll do it.

CARL:  No, no, listen, why don't you play tonight? In our game, here, you'll clean up.

ASH:  Clean up? In a baby's game. What do I win? A packet of smarties.

CARL:  There's money here, there's money I promise. They're all shit. Mugsy lost three grand a month ago. Sometimes the game goes mental, everyone goes on tilt.

ASH:  You think there's four grand here?

CARL:  Maybe not four, three maybe, two definitely.

ASH:  I need four.

CARL:  There's four, there's four. How much do you owe?

ASH:  Ten.

**Beat.**

CARL:  How much have you got?

ASH:  Five, plus your fucking 'four'.

CARL (*close*):  Please. Come on . . . you're a professional . . . it's easy money . . . you're brilliant . . . you're the best . . .

**Pause.**

ASH:  Who's playing?

CARL:  Me, Mugsy, Sweeney – plays like a madman, can't pass, pure aggression, no brains. Dad, granite . . . just push the right buttons he's easy. And Frankie, he's quite good.

ASH:  What does that mean?

CARL:  He's a bit flash, likes to mix it up.

ASH:  And he's quite good?

CARL:  In this game yeah but you'll kill him. Please. Help.

**Beat.**

**ASH takes out his mobile phone. He exits. CARL is left alone in the restaurant.**

**Kitchen.**

**Enter SWEENEY and FRANKIE.**

SWEENEY:  So where you going, Butlins?

FRANKIE (*holding an airline ticket*):  Las Vegas mate, the States. US of A.

SWEENEY:  When?

FRANKIE: It's an open ticket, soon as I've saved enough money, couple of months.

SWEENEY: To do what?

FRANKIE: Play poker.

SWEENEY: You? Turn professional poker player?

FRANKIE: Yeah . . . why not?

**Pause.**

SWEENEY: Because . . . but it doesn't mean you have to . . . what about . . . everything here?

FRANKIE: What here?

SWEENEY: Here . . . I dunno, me . . . Mugsy . . .

FRANKIE: You can come and visit me in my five-star suite at Caesar's Palace. I'll lay on some broads.

**Beat.**

SWEENEY: I shouldn't play tonight.

FRANKIE: You said you'd play . . . I mean . . . don't play if you don't want to.

SWEENEY: I don't want to let the boys down.

FRANKIE: Play for a while, see how it goes . . .

SWEENEY: You want my money?

FRANKIE: No . . . Yeah.

SWEENEY: So how much you got saved Frank?

FRANKIE: A few grand, one big win and I'm sorted. I'm going Sween, there's no way I'm not going. I've got the ticket Sween. I've been saying for years I'm going to leave this shithole.

SWEENEY: What shithole?

FRANKIE: This place, London, England, everywhere. This country's a shanty town. It's dead Sween.

SWEENEY: So go to Vegas.

**Restaurant.**

**ASH enters and puts his mobile on the table.**

ASH: You're lucky.

CARL: Thanks.

ASH: Three hours and that's it, I go to your father.

CARL: Thank you.

**Beat.**

ASH: Why d'you piss me about?

CARL: I haven't done it on purpose.

ASH: What about all the meals at the casino? The money? The drinks, the late nights, the cabs. I've given you my time. I taught you how to play poker. I've covered your debts for a year. I trusted you and you repay me like . . .

**Beat.**

ASH: You're compulsive.

CARL: And you're not?

ASH: No, only thing I'm addicted to is these. (*He holds up his cigarette.*)

CARL: Actually, can I have one?

**Beat.**

ASH: Fuck off, get your own.

CARL: Come on, don't be like my dad.

ASH: I'm not like your dad Carl – I don't care about you.

**Pause.**

CARL: I thought you liked me?

**Beat.**

ASH: Not especially.

**Pause.**

CARL: Why do you . . . why did you let me play in your game?

ASH: The big boys' game?

CARL: Yes.

ASH: Cos you're a mug. You're value.

**Pause.**

CARL: So . . . if you don't like me, why don't you go to him now and get the money . . . what is this?

**Beat.**

ASH: Pity.

CARL: You pity me?
ASH: No, your father.

**Pause.**

CARL: Who shall I say you are?
ASH: What do you mean?
CARL: I can't say this is Ash, he's a professional poker player, is it OK if he sits down and takes your money.
ASH: Say what you like . . . it's your problem.
CARL: Your my teacher, ex-teacher.
ASH: From where?
CARL: School.
ASH: What a fucking mess.

# david spencer

## from *Hurricane Roses*

David Spencer was born in Halifax and lives in Berlin. He is the author of the following plays: *Releevo* (Soho Poly), *Space* (Cottesloe/Soho Poly), *Blue Hearts* (RNT Studio), *Killing the Cat* (Royal Court Theatre Upstairs), *The Land of the Living* (Royal Court Theatre Upstairs) and *Hurricane Roses* (RNT Studio).

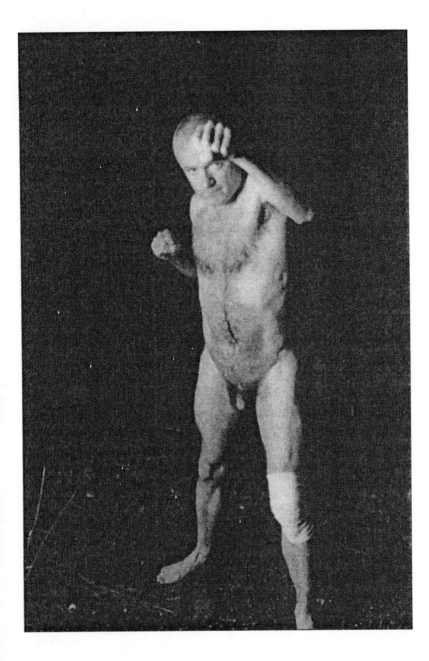

**JEAN moves slowly towards TYLER.**

JEAN: If that doctor tells me I'm to lose my legs. You won't be seeing me! / That's no threat. That's a fact. / Am tellin yee. Y'wont be seeing me. Ever. You hear me?

**Tyler turns from JEAN.**

JEAN: Have you been drinkin?
TYLER: **Have I been drinking?**
JEAN: Have you been drinkin?
TYLER (*laughing*): Have I been drinkin?
JEAN: Have you been drinkin?
TYLER: **Have I been drinking?**
JEAN (*overlap*): The bloody image of your father.
TYLER: Tell me news.
JEAN (*overlap*): Now listen to me!
TYLER: News?
JEAN (*overlap*): Have you been drinkin?
TYLER: **News!**
JEAN (*overlap*): Tyler!
TYLER: And here. Two hours too early.
JEAN (*overlap*): Have you been drinkin?
TYLER: Cuz a'll be pissed by nine.
JEAN: Tyler . . .

**JEAN slowly into darkness as . . .**

TYLER: The Nine O'Clock News. / Millions starve as Amiland gobs half the World's food. Juicy Flesh do Death Burgers for less than the price of a pack a recycled bog roll. Economic rationality! And **has Tyler been drinking?** Utopian Socialist vision crammed down wi'owt a dying belch. (*American accent.*) **Told you Reds Central Planning won't work. See son. Force's the thing. Market force**. / Self-esteem pissed at n'longer being a super power. The British ruling class indulge in a bitta bullying a'Thick Micks an' assorted Wogs. / Germany says t'the EEC. Wall up Life Boat Europe. And if niggers. Slant eyes. Or any other non-Aryan gook tries to get in. Shoot the bastard. / And tonight's summary. Is Body Earth Terminal? Lungs fucked. Fluids poisoned. Skin punctured. And **has Tyler been drinking?**

**JEAN, claw-handed, palms pills she swills down with brandy. She conceals**

**the brandy and the pills.**

TYLER: And now a funny at the end. Earlier this morning a plane crashed into Buckingham Palarse. / Wait for it! / A Palarse Spokesperson said the four hundred passengers died. **Almost**. Instantly. / **Our** Princess McDee. Wearing a tasteful blue coat with a tasteful white lace trim and a tasteful orange hat. Was visiting the Palarse on a recently obtained Westminster County Council care order. **Our Tastefulness** finished her **Cornflakes**. And before walking tastefully away. Spat in **Charley**'s dead eye. / I miss you Mum! I miss you Mum.

**JEAN can't turn on the music player.**
**Lightning.**

TYLER: I remember that clinic waiting room like it were yesterday. All those couples holding hands and talking in low voices. All smiles and togetherness. Like we were in some airport lounge. Waiting to go on a mass honeymoon. And that fish tank. Do you remember that fuckin fish tank?

JUDITH: **You drain me!**

TYLER: I couldn't get the idea owtta me head. That the embryo in you had gills too. And the fish in that tank were water-cherubs wi'wings n'gills. I shudda screamed my fucking head off. **No! Don't do it! Don't do it!**

JUDITH: Look at it from where we are now.

TYLER: That's when I started crying. And you said.

JUDITH (*overlap*): It would have made things a lot lot harder!

TYLER (*overlap*): **I shudda come with Emma. / I shudda come with Emma.**

JUDITH: I need someone to care for me sometimes.

TYLER: Oh very good Judith. You're very good at saying **This is what Judith wants. This is what Judith feels.** But do you ever show me what you want. What you feel?

JUDITH: You're talking about yourself!

TYLER: Oh am I? Am I really? You were empty Judith. Empty but for a great big howl. And if I did pump into you. If I did just empty my balls. It was because I wanted to fill you up with me. Just fuck away the loss.

JUDITH: Why didn't you say anything?

TYLER: Why didn't you?

JUDITH: I did what was right.

TYLER: And that's what really hurt.

JUDITH: It was right. For Christssake Tyler. It was right.

TYLER: I know it was right! Judith's choice I said. Judith's right. Tyler's a fuck up. / All that rational shite about **wrong time. Something to cling to. Eventually we will**. / I felt like everything we'd been up to then had come to a leap you didn't trust to take with me. / You say you want someone to care for you. But do you dont mean me!

JUDITH: If I ever did reach out to you. You were either busy with your own need. Drunk. Or worse. Dragged my arm out at the socket!

**Silence.**

TYLER: Did Mum tell you about John? Grandma wanned Mum to have an abortion.

JUDITH: **She gave her the money to go to London.**

TYLER: But Mum had him anyway. My Uncle said. **Shud she bring that bastard home. I'll drown it!** And me Grandma? **Give him away or dont come home. Pure Patriarchy there?** / Y'suppose that wudda scarred me Mum?

JUDITH: You can't just haul out the past. If . . .

TYLER (cuts in): **Well Mum? Seems y'can't haul out the past. We will all be forgotten. Such indeed is our fate. Nowt we can do about it. What we find serious . . .**

JUDITH (cuts in swiftly): **Significant highly important. The time will come when it's all forgotten.**

TYLER: I'm sorry I taught you that.

JUDITH: **Can you just drop the Jesus Christ act? Can you? / What I mean is. If all you do with the past is carve yourself up. It's useless to you. Sooner or later you've to live for** the future.

TYLER: It's the present we live in.

JUDITH: Philosophical bullshit!

TYLER: Life is a lot harder than **cheer up.**

JUDITH: **Yeah. And Jean knew that as well as anybody!** But despite all the crap. You make the future mean something to you. And you live for it! / It was her work. Not becuz she couldn't move. May be not **even** the pain. It was her work. It was . . .

TYLER (cuts in): She O.D.'d whilst she were at work! Me and ower Trish scraped enough **Valium** out of her mouth t'kill an army. A ten year old boy. A seven year old girl? There were times I wished her dead!

JUDITH: You didn't. I know you didn't. And I'm sure Jean didn't either.

TYLER: What are you at Judith?

JUDITH: I'm trying to help you.

TYLER: Mum dint mean it?

JUDITH: Trying to share an insight.

TYLER (*overlap*): That it was a mistake? / She took her own life.

JUDITH: And how does that make **you** feel. / FOR CHRISTSSAKE TYLER WHAT THE FUCK DO YOU FEEL!

TYLER: FUCKED OFF! AND WHEN I'M FUCKED OFF ENOUGH. I'D GO AS FAR AS T'SAY. THIS POXY STATE THIS POXY COUNTRY. IT FUCKING MADE HER MANGLED HER AND IT FUCKING MURDERED HER!

**Silence.**

JUDITH: What I was trying to say was . . . I was just saying. / **Tyler**.

**JUDITH inclines to touching TYLER but does not touch him.**

JUDITH: After Jean's first stomach pump. She was in hospital a few days for treatment.

TYLER: Likely more drugs.

JUDITH: **Listen**. Y'know it wasn't her first attempt. But the others were **cries for help**. Her words. Anyway. She wouldn't go home in an ambulance. **The neighbours**. She got a taxi. But only rode 'round the corner. / It was spring. I know from how she said. **The light green buds all opening on the trees**. / A woman stopped Jean and asked. **Can I help?** She noticed Jean was embarrassed and said. **I had to ask you looked so dead sad.** Jean never forgot how a total stranger stopped in the street. And asked. **Can I help you?**

TYLER: She told me the same story!

JUDITH (*choked up*): I remember her face as she said.

TYLER: It's the **why I wanted to be a nurse story**.

JUDITH (*overlap*): **That's when I decided to be a nurse**. / (*Choked up*.) It's vivid because she said. **You'll be the only one who'll understand. You're like me. It does y'good to help other people.**

TYLER: **You'll be the only one who understands me. You're like me. It's why y'do all that political stuff. Isn't it?**

JUDITH: So she repeated herself? / At the party the nurses gave. When she couldn't go back. Alice the MP. Alice said when the arthritis set in. Though Jean was still at work. She was in the most pain ever. The pain killers were low grade. Every move was an act of faith. She clenched and smiled and kept on.

TYLER (*overlap*): Romantic bullshit. Cleaning arses.

JUDITH (*overlap*): It was really central to her.

TYLER: Stripping corpses n'stitching up drunks. Does not bring fulfillment. She worked for money!

JUDITH: Oh I know she worked for money. And I know that the demands of that kind of work brings its own dangers. But I also think helping other people brought Jean meaning.

TYLER: Self justification **Judith**.

JUDITH: Empathy **Tyler!** / I think right up until . . .

TYLER (*cuts in*): She was depressed!

JUDITH: **I think right up until the** . . .

TYLER (*cuts in*): She was always depressed!

**TV screen:**
**No smoking. / Hospital video surveillance**.

JUDITH: **I think** . . .

TYLER (*cuts in*): This time she had something to be depressed about.

**HAROLD on the waiting room bench. He'd like a fag but . . . He coughs.**

JUDITH: **Right up until the last moment**. She hoped she'd get back to work. When she saw she wouldn't . . .

**JEAN enters very very slowly.**

HAROLD: What did he say luv? What did that doctor say?

JEAN: I'm not being pushed around in any old wheelchair.

HAROLD: Here luv. (*Gives her his seat.*) What did he say? What he say?

JEAN: He said. **If I dont stop smoking. I'm gonna lose my legs**.

HAROLD: Just like that? / **Rite. I'm off to see him!**

JEAN: **Dont!**

HAROLD: I've always thought he were a rite ignorant sod anyroad!

JEAN: **Dont do that**.

**HAROLD goes far away from JEAN. JEAN tries to take a cig from her packet.**

HAROLD (*calls*):  Hey up you! / Never mind five bloody minutes!

**Sound: A war helicopter passes overhead.**
**JEAN drops her fags, covers her ears.**

HAROLD (*coughs*):  A dont give a shit how many sick patients you've t'see.
A've me wife owt ere in tears! Am next on that list! No ifs. No buts. /
Y'just tell him Harry Norman'll have words we him. / Aye. And thank
you very much and all.

**HAROLD returns to JEAN. He sees her cigarettes and picks them up.**

HAROLD:  Y'come on back in we me! We'll sort that bloody fella owt! If
it costs me another 'artattack. (*Cough*.) I'll belt his nose 'til it opens up
like a bloody purse.
JEAN:  I need a by-pass.
HAROLD:  Don't cry luv.
JEAN:  Those things only last a few years at best.
HAROLD:  We'll get us a second opinion.
JEAN:  A mean if a did stop.
HAROLD:  There'll be summat we can do.

**HAROLD coughs.**

JEAN:  They dont last.
HAROLD:  A promise y'luv.

**Awkward but profound, HAROLD embraces JEAN, him standing, her sitting.**

JEAN:  A few years then that's it!
HAROLD:  They said you wunt get (*Cough*.) Your Mobility. But y'got it!
JEAN:  I dont wanna go on we no legs.

**Sound: 'Mr Harold Norman. To F2 Room F417. Please.'**

JEAN:  I dont wannt go on we no legs.

**Silence.**
**Sound: 'Mr Harold Norman. To F2 Room F417. Please.'**
**HAROLD coughs.**
**Sound: 'Thank you.'**

JEAN: There's no way I'm going on without legs.

**Lightning.**

JUDITH: In England five per cent of men. And **ten** per cent of women. Are at some time depressive. **Fifteen per cent** by some definitions.

TYLER: How's it your theories have to stake claim to everything.

JUDITH: They're not my theories.

TYLER: Do a feminist analysis of elephant hunting. Be a laugh that!

JUDITH (*overlap*): They're something I do my work with. It's like you bringing acid home from the lab to clean the kettle.

TYLER: Limescale equals suicide? And y'dont wannt talk nutso equations. **Fucking marvellous**. Go off up the Centre n'save the World.

JUDITH: Bit uncomfortable?

TYLER: Or fuck Emma.

JUDITH: Bit emotional.

TYLER (*overlap*): Or whatever y'do do up there?

JUDITH: Tyler gets afraid! Wants to run away. Typical.

TYLER: When **typical** means common or normal. It's normal to want t'run from what y'fear. **Fear flight fight!** But since it's **typical you** to use **typical** t'mean **typically male!** Tell me this. If women are so good at talking emotion. How come more get depressed?

JUDITH: I don't know.

TYLER: **You dont know**.

JUDITH: But as you say. The first thing to do with what you fear is get away from it. But women. Quite neurotically. Are socialized to cope with fear.

TYLER (*overlap*): **What are you on about?**

JUDITH: And if they do need to fight are they taught to hit back?

TYLER (*overlap*): WHAT ARE YOU ON ABOUT?

JUDITH (*overlap*): No! They're taught to turn aggression in on themselves. And **that's depression**.

TYLER: WHAT THE FUCK ARE YOU ON ABOUT!

JUDITH: Tom!

TYLER: / Mum's been away from Dad for years now.

JUDITH: Not really.

TYLER: Years!

JUDITH: You said yourself **Mum's still in love with Dad**. At first I thought it was cuz you wanned that. But now I think you were right.

Y'dont just walk away from twenty years. You were there. Your Trish . . .

TYLER: You're talking like Harry didn't exist.

JUDITH: Harry's one of the best things ever t'happen to your Mum. A sweet simple ordinary bloke. But precisely because he is sweet simple and ordinary. He wasn't equipped to help her. Not in the end. It takes a special kind of person to go that far.

TYLER: You maybe?

JUDITH: You maybe? / Harry couldn't cope.

TYLER: You dont know what it's like to live we someone who every second week tells you they're gunna do themselves in.

JUDITH: Nothing like every second week. Often I grant you. But on a scale of years and not weeks.

TYLER: She drove Harry himself to an'overdose.

JUDITH: In a relationship with someone like Jean. **Attempted suicide becomes a means of communication**.

TYLER: / When me and our Trish were kids we called it. **The Suicide Game**. We used to think she played it for attention!

JUDITH: She probably did. Probably saying. **Look. Look at me**. I'm trapped in this horrible relationship! And I stay because **I love you kids. Help me!**

TYLER: Y'mek it sound s'one sided. I loved me Mum! But she could be bloody evil. Me Dad worked his balls off! Sent us on 'oliday every year. Put me and Trish through college. An' for what? Money for bosses n'taxes to a state that dunt give a fuck about workers at the end of their working life!

JUDITH: Why do you think your Dad worked so often away from home?

TYLER: To get away from me Mum! / Dont look at me like that! He said it often enough!

JUDITH: It is certainly true that when someone causes stress in a relationship it often comes back on them.

TYLER: **You just drop that fuckin tone. You just shut the fuck up now. Cuz you dont know what you're talking about**. / Yer so fuckin judgmental. It's a wonder you can do the kind work you do do.

**Silence.**

JUDITH: Your Mum wanted to leave for years **but thought she had to**

**stay for the kids**. She probably thought by sending him away he could work and drink.

TYLER: There was no work in Halifax!

JUDITH: And she could try to protect you all from the worst of it.

TYLER: And the money was better!

JUDITH: Was she happier if he wasn't there?

TYLER: Me Mum loved me Dad.

JUDITH: Just ask yourself.

TYLER: There were times he cud be a bastard.

JUDITH: Were you happier?

TYLER: But he was always a very lovable bastard. And Mum loved him.

JUDITH: If y'love someone it's hard t'stop loving no matter what they do. That's the trap! Women start to see where they are as normal. In extreme cases they cease to struggle because they're exhausted by fear.

TYLER: He wern't one a these beating her every week types.

JUDITH: There often are long quiet periods. Your Mum probably believed it wouldn't happen again. Trouble is it always does.

TYLER: An' odd slap in a row that mostly she'd start. It was always him who felt shit. He'd be guilt ridden for months. And she'd grind him. Grind him! Cuz she had him where she wanted him.

JUDITH: He kicked her whilst she was pregnant.

TYLER: Who told you that?

JUDITH: Jean told me.

TYLER: / Wun night. **He were drunk**. It wer late. But he were singing. **Happy Birthday**. An he put a bottle a brandy down on't coffee table. And Mum said. **Tom I told yee not to bring drink in the house**. And he kept on singing. **Happy Birthday**. Just singing. And she picked up the bottle. And she hit him in the head we it! Did she tell you this one? / He sat there on the couch. Blood pouring off his face. Blood tears and brandy running down his face. And he said. **The brandy was for you Jean**. And she said. **It's two o'clock Tom. My Birthday was yesterday**. Me and our Trish hant given her owt. We'd forgot. / Me Dad put his wage packet on the coffee table. And he went tert bathroom t'clean himself up. And Mum turned to me. And she said. **There yee are now Tyler. There yee are. Now you see what he's really like**. She tell y'that did she?

JUDITH: He kicked her more than once.

TYLER: My Dad was a hard man.

JUDITH: And he tried to strangle her.

TYLER: If he'd wanted to beat someone up. They'd not get up again.

JUDITH: Just listen to yourself.

TYLER: **Never mind me listening t'meself**.

JUDITH: That's the reality of the threat.

TYLER: **You listen t'me** / She would demand the impossible. I feel terrible talking about her like this. But look at the way she were wi'Harry. She'd only ever want what he cunt give her.

JUDITH: That's not true.

TYLER: The time with the decorating. She went on and on and it lucced OK. But whilst she were out. A man we two heart attacks. Got on a step ladder t'wall-paper. / It weren't a brilliant job. But instead a seeing he'd done his best. She just told him it wern't good enough. Worse. Teld him **me Dad were good at decorating!** She knew who's side I were on there. I'll tell yer. She wunt talk t'me for months!

JUDITH: I'm not saying y'Dad was the ultimate thug. But Jean was a victim. Once violence enters a relationship. It becomes a currency. And it's very very difficult to eradicate.

TYLER: **Where's this going?**

**TYLER goes for a bottle. JUDITH, aware of the risk, follows and keeps on.**

JUDITH: If you've a drunk who's trying t'crush your neck.

TYLER: She is dead and she meant it!

JUDITH: Then you've an event! A woman in a violent relationship is in a jungle of such events. A squabble about washing up. What time someone comes in. The sexual act even. The dynamic's always the same. And everything is defined by the clearest manifest. In this case the murder crazed drunk. Living twenty years with that threat will scar!

TYLER: Y'know we're not talking feeling here Judith. This is anatomy. Y'expect me t'hack out vital organs n'take a detached look. It hurts! **It hurts me!** / And you can turn that last lot on its head! Y'live with a suicidal woman who y'love very much. But can't cope with her continual threats of self destruction! Watta yer do? Leaving isn't easy! An' even if y'do. You've the feeling you can't out run it. So watta y'do? Amateur anatomy Judith. Y'destroy the threat. Perhaps Dad was just desperately trying to help her along a bit.

JUDITH (*not accusatively*): Is that why you told her she should do it?

TYLER: / You bitch!

**Silence.**

**JEAN claw-hard hands, downs tablets and brandy and hides the
remainder.**

TYLER: I told her. I told her she should stop threatening people who
loved her. I mainly meant Harry. And then I told her. That if she really
meant it. Then it were her decision. That I loved her. And that I would
miss her!

**Silence.**

# helen edmundson
## from *The Clearing*

Helen Edmundson was born in Liverpool in 1964. She is the author of: *Flying* (RNT Studio, 1990), *The Clearing* (Bush Theatre, 1993) – winner of the John Whiting Award – and *Coventry Carol* (Hampstead Theatre, 1995). Her adaptations of *Anna Karenina* (1992) and *The Mill on the Floss* (1994) for Shared Experience both won *Time Out* Awards and she is currently adapting *War and Peace* for the RNT's Olivier Theatre.

**Autumn 1655. County Kildare, Ireland. The authorities have permitted Englishman ROBERT PRESTON to retain his farm while ordering his Irish Catholic wife MADELEINE to be transplanted to Connaught. She, however, has run away with their baby son Ralph to join the rebels led by Pierce Kinsellagh. ROBERT has vowed to track them down.**

**In a clearing, in a wood.**
**It is a misty, howling evening. From one side of the clearing, a voice comes.**

ROBERT:  Madeleine Preston? Are you there?

**From the other side, a voice answers.**

MADELEINE:  My name is Maddy O'Hart.
ROBERT:  Are you alone and unarmed?
MADELEINE:  I am.
Are you alone and unarmed?
ROBERT:  I am.
Have you brought the child?

**Pause.**

ROBERT:  Step out into the clearing and I will step out.

**Slowly, through the mist, MADELEINE and ROBERT emerge. They stop, several paces from each other.**

ROBERT:  I knew you would not refuse me.
A soldier thought he saw you once. A woman and a child, swimming in the Slaney, laughing. She ran. Was it you?
I have searched, this last year, for sight or sound of you. You disappeared into the air. I questioned every man we took.
I offered a reward for Pierce Kinsellagh in the hope that he might lead me to you.
MADELEINE:  We do not sell our own. You should know that by now.
The man who brought your message . . .
ROBERT:  It won him his life.
MADELEINE:  He said you work for Sturman.
ROBERT:  I work for my country.
MADELEINE:  I hope you are happy, Robert. I have tried to picture you happy.

**Pause.**

**There is a sound from amongst the trees on ROBERT's side of the clearing.**

ROBERT: Wolves.

Let me see Ralph now.

MADELEINE: Tell me of Solomon and Susaneh. I have looked for them many times amongst the people on the highway.

ROBERT: They do not go. Protestants are exempt now on payment of a fine. Madeleine . . .

MADELEINE: I am glad for them.

Tell them . . . Please tell them I will never forget their kindness.

ROBERT: Madeleine, let Ralph come forward now.

I have longed to see him. You cannot know how much.

Let him come here to me. I have presents for his birthday.

MADELEINE: Ralph is dead.

He died five weeks ago.

ROBERT: Dead?

It is his birthday.

MADELEINE: He is dead.

He came and saw the way things are and went away again.

ROBERT: No. You are lying.

MADELEINE: I have learnt to lie, Robert, but I would not lie with this. I do not want to hurt you. I only came to tell you he is dead. All the people that knew and it was only you I wanted.

ROBERT: This is evil. In truth. He has been asking for me, hasn't he? You think I will go away and leave him alone.

MADELEINE: No.

ROBERT: You think to keep him from me.

(*Calling.*) Ralph.

Ralph, it is your father. Come to me, Ralph.

MADELEINE: Why do you think I came here? I came because I knew you would not believe me and I wanted you to see it in my eyes. Look at my eyes, Robert. He is dead. It is over.

**Pause.**

MADELEINE: We did some fine destructive work between us.

ROBERT: You killed him. If you had not taken him from me . . . if you had not taken him he would not have . . .

MADELEINE: And why did I take him? Tell me the choice. No. No, this isn't it.

ROBERT: What then? You're doing this . . . You're the one who comes here saying he is . . .

MADELEINE: Blame me if you will. But it's the truth.

**She moves her hand.**

ROBERT: Don't move. I'm warning you.

**She slowly pulls a toy from her cloak and holds it out to him.**
**He does not move. She throws it gently across to him.**

MADELEINE: You chose it for him. It was his favourite. He would want for you to have it.

ROBERT **looks at it, then crouches and picks it up.**

MADELEINE: He was strong and happy while we lived in the woods. But soldiers came to fell the trees, forced us back to lower ground. There was fever there. He cried a lot and died.

ROBERT: Oh my God, he is dead.

**He begins to sob silently.**

ROBERT: What have I lost? What have I lost?

MADELEINE: Robert?

We are finished now. There is nothing left between us.

Perhaps that is good. I have even found a sort of peace. Everything is very simple. I hope you find it too.

ROBERT: You bitch.

MADELEINE: What?

ROBERT: You Irish bitch. If only I had known that's what it takes to make you happy, to watch your child die, to whore it with barbarians, to kill and terrorise and . . .

MADELEINE: You're wrong.

ROBERT: I'm glad I kill you. I'm glad I kill you all. All of you.

**There is shame behind his eyes.**

MADELEINE: Nothing you can say will touch me.

I do what I do because I have to and because I hope that one day, the people who come after me will have their lives for themselves without this pulling back and pulling back. That they will have their lives to fly like falcons, off their hands and back again as they will. It is a dream. And I will not give it up.

The only thing I can't forgive you for, the only thing, is that you would not see the strength you had beside you, right beside you. And you would not hold me by the hand and walk forward with me to take our lives.

I loved you, and would have loved you always. Always.

Maybe that was not enough.

**She takes out a piece of paper and holds it out.**

MADELEINE: It is a map that shows his grave. You will want to go and see him.

**He walks towards her and takes it. They look into each other's eyes. She reaches out and touches his face. He lets her.**
**Pause.**

MADELEINE: What happens now, Robert?

I turn around to walk and find a bullet in my back?

ROBERT: What do you mean?

MADELEINE: I have lived beneath the sky a while now and it has taught me many things. Almost as canny as Killaine, I am. And I have learnt the difference between the sound of wolves and the sound of men with guns. You are not alone. You have your people with you.

ROBERT: Yes.

MADELEINE: And I have mine.

**The lights dim. There is the sound of a hundred guns being cocked. The lights are gone.**

**The End.**

# acknowledgements

The editor makes grateful acknowledgement to the following for permission to reprint extracts from previously published material:

Faber and Faber Ltd for *The Present* from *Nick Ward: Plays 1* © Nick Ward 1995. Flood Books for *Cat and Mouse (Sheep)* from *Plays* © Gregory Motton 1995. Nick Hern Books for *The Clearing* © Helen Edmundson 1994 and *The Strip* © Phyllis Nagy 1995. Methuen Drama for *Indian Summer* from *Making Scenes 3* © Harwant Bains 1995, for *A Vision of Love Revealed in Sleep (Part Three)* from *Gay Plays: Four* © Neil Bartlett 1990, for *The Lodger* © Simon Burke 1994, for *Can't Stand Up For Falling Down* © Richard Cameron 1991, for *Beautiful Thing* © Jonathan Harvey 1994, for *Somewhere* from *Frontline Intelligence I* © Judith Johnson 1993, for *Blasted* from *Frontline Intelligence II* © Sarah Kane 1994, for *Dealer's Choice* © Patrick Marber 1995, for *Some Voices* from *Frontline Intelligence III* © Joe Penhall 1995, for *The Fastest Clock in the Universe* © Philip Ridley 1992 and for *Hurricane Roses* from *Frontline Intelligence II* © David Spencer 1994. Oberon Books Ltd for *The Neighbour* (ISBN 1 870259 31 9) © Meredith Oakes 1993.

And to the authors for permission to print previously unpublished material: extracts from *Happy Land West* © Kate Dean 1996; from *Neville Southall's Washbag* © David Farr 1996; from *Fearquest* © Paul Godfrey 1996; and from *Revolver* © Emily Woof 1996.

## Methuen Modern Plays

*include work by*

Jean Anouilh
John Arden
Margaretta D'Arcy
Peter Barnes
Sebastian Barry
Brendan Behan
Edward Bond
Bertolt Brecht
Howard Brenton
Simon Burke
Jim Cartwright
Caryl Churchill
Noël Coward
Sarah Daniels
Nick Dear
Shelagh Delaney
David Edgar
Dario Fo
Michael Frayn
John Godber
Paul Godfrey
John Guare
Peter Handke
Jonathan Harvey
Iain Heggie
Declan Hughes
Terry Johnson
Barrie Keeffe
Stephen Lowe

Doug Lucie
John McGrath
David Mamet
Patrick Marber
Arthur Miller
Mtwa, Ngema & Simon
Tom Murphy
Peter Nichols
Joseph O'Connor
Joe Orton
Louise Page
Joe Penhall
Luigi Pirandello
Stephen Poliakoff
Franca Rame
Philip Ridley
David Rudkin
Willy Russell
Jean-Paul Sartre
Sam Shepard
Wole Soyinka
C. P. Taylor
Theatre de Complicite
Theatre Workshop
Sue Townsend
Judy Upton
Timberlake Wertenbaker
Victoria Wood

For a Complete Catalogue of Methuen Drama titles
write to:

Methuen Drama
Michelin House
81 Fulham Road
London SW3 6RB